A HOLISTIC PROTOCOL

for the

IMMUNE SYSTEM

Disclaimer

Neither the author nor the publisher of this book is in any way connected with the health food manufacturing or retailing industries, actively or inactively. The publisher does not sell vitamins or other supplements which are recommended or mentioned in this book. Neither author nor publisher owns or operates any health food stores.

The author does not directly or indirectly dispense medical advice, diagnose or prescribe. He offers health information that the reader can consider, in cooperation with his chosen health specialist, who should be consulted first. He does not claim that this protocol is the ultimate answer to AIDS or any other immune-suppressed disease. This protocol is being continually refined and updated.

The author and publisher are not stating that the use of any products described in this book will cure AIDS or any other disease. Information on the supplements in this book has been derived from the best professional sources.

In the event that the reader uses this information without a health practitioner's approval, he is prescribing for himself, which is his constitutional right, but the author and the publisher assume no responsibility.

© Copyright, 1989 Tree of Life Publications

Tree of Life Publications
P. O. Box 126
Joshua Tree, CA 92252

Printed in the United States of America
First Printing August 1989; Revised, April, 1990
Third edition, updated, March, 1991
Fourth edition, updated, January, 1992
    10 9 8 7 6 5 4

Library of Congress Cataloging-in-Publication Data

Gregory, Scott J.
    A Holistic Protocol for the Immune System

    AIDS (Disease)—Alternative treatment. 2. Opportunistic
infections—Alternative treatment. I. Leonardo, Bianca.
II. Title. [DNLM: 1. AIDS-Related Complex—therapy.
2. Epstein-Barr—therapy. 3. Candidiasis—therapy.
4. Herpes—therapy. 5. Opportunistic Infections—
therapy. WD 308 G823p]
RC607.A26G757 1989   616.97'9206   89-20310
ISBN: 0-930852-18-4 (pbk.)

A HOLISTIC PROTOCOL

for the

IMMUNE SYSTEM

HIV/ARC/AIDS

CANDIDIASIS • EPSTEIN-BARR • HERPES

And Other Opportunistic Infections

Scott J. Gregory, O.M.D.

Bianca Leonardo, Editor

DEDICATION

In the spirit of enlightenment:

To medical doctors and other health professionals

—who want to try something new — that works!

And to patients who want to help themselves.

CONTENTS

The "New" or Holistic Medicine vii

Immuno-Suppressed? viii

General Treatment Principles ix

The Four Categories Explained x

Chapter   Page

   I.   Detailed Descriptions of Protocol..11

   II.   HIV "Positive" to "Negative" is Possible..41

   III.   Commonalities Among AIDS Survivors 45

   IV.   Opportunistic Infections and Associated Diseases: HIV/ARC/AIDS 47

   V.   Opportunistic Infections: CANDIDIASIS 55

   VI.   Opportunistic Infections: EPSTEIN-BARR 61

   VII.   Opportunistic Infections: HERPES I and II; HEPATITIS B (HBV) 63

   VIII.   Opportunistic Infections: CYTOMEGALOVIRUS (CMV)........66

   IX.   Opportunistic Infections: KAPOSI'S SARCOMA (KS)......................68

   X.   Opportunistic Infections: PNEUMOCYSTIS PNEUMONIA (PCP)..............70

   XI.   Opportunistic Infections: STAPHYLOCOCCUS and STREPTOCOCCUS 73

   XII.   New Perspectives..76

Index 86

NATIONAL HEALTH ALERT!!

"Hepatitis A" Spread by Contaminated Fruits and Vegetables
—A Major Health Hazard

Epidemics and periodic outbreaks of hepatitis and dysentery are becoming more and more widespread in the U. S.

Hepatitis A, Salmonella, E. Coli, the dysentery-producing *Shigella bacteria, Giardia lamblia*, and *Entamoeba Histolytica* are the most common germs (viruses, parasites, bacteria and fungi) found infecting the fresh fruits and vegetables in local store produce sections, restaurants and salad bars.

In Louisville, more than 220 people were sickened with hepatitis A. Nearly one fourth were hospitalized; two people died from the infection, one after $1 million in medical expenses and a liver transplant. The Centers for Disease Control concluded that lettuce was the culprit, since everyone who got sick at the restaurants had eaten lettuce that was contaminated before it reached Louisville.

The C.D.C. investigators discovered that the lettuce arrived in unopened cases and was sent directly to restaurants, unwashed and unprocessed. The source of the contamination was the growing field.

Between field and table, someone infected with the hepatitis virus had touched the lettuce. But where to start? Upwards of 2.5 million farm workers harvest the nation's food, many of them carriers of infectious diseases. Farm workers are poorer and sicker than almost any other segment of the U. S. population. And they have to work regardless of whether they are sick or not.

Dr. Jesse Ortiz, professor of public health at the University of Massachusetts, one of the nation's experts on migrant health, told the Department of Labor four years ago that the rate of hepatitis among farm workers is extremely high—331 times greater than that of the general population. The disease is so rampant that by adulthood nearly 90 percent of farm workers have been sickened by it. These people have very limited access to health care.

Every American eats an average of 25.7 pounds of lettuce yearly. Those delicate perishable leaves link the cleanest of kitchens to the teeming *colonias* of south Texas, the squalid fields of western Mexico, and the temporary migrant camps improvised throughout the state of California. A contaminated head of lettuce could be harvested, shipped and eaten long before many of its hitchhiking hepatitis virus particles die.

What Can You Do?

(1) Contact your congressman and senators to initiate action on this scandal. This serious, national health problem will require congressional action. Also write to: House Committee on Agriculture, 1301 Longworth, House Office Building, Washington, D. C. 20510.

(2) Cook your raw foods, whenever possible. Temperatures above 140° F. are needed to kill hepatitis A.

(3) Wash all produce that is eaten raw. First remove all outer leaves from vegetables like lettuce and cabbage. Soak your fruits and vegetables in a sink full of water with several drops of NutriBiotic (available in health food stores, or call (800) 225-4345, Customer Service). It contains a biologically active botanical extract of citrus proven to effectively control numerous germs (including viruses and bacteria).

(4) Until this national health hazard is remedied, you could refuse to purchase or consume produce from the supermarkets, or eat from restaurant salad bars. For home use, purchase organic produce from small, organic growers. Health food stores are one source. One enterprising company will ship organic produce to your home via U. P. S., to any location, with no minimum quantity required. They are: Diamond Organics, 800-922-2396. They are in Freedom, California. Claim your freedom from contaminated produce; protect yourself and your family.

As this book was going to press, the editor was alerted to this news story by reading the publication "Body & Soul, Your Health and Fitness Guide," UNIC, P. O. Box 610, Carmichael, CA 95609. We thank them for permission to use this news of great import to the American public.

An Invitation to Explore and Experience

The "New" or Holistic Medicine

Immune Suppression is the new health problem of the '90s, after surfacing with the epidemic of AIDS in the '80s.

What are the causes? What is the solution?

The author and publisher present their third work in this field, from the standpoint of "The New Medicine." New? Only in the sense of being rediscovered. It is actually 2400 years old.

Hippocrates, called "The Father of Medicine," lived in ancient Greece about 400 B.C. "He stated that the body heals itself with some help. This is a basic tenet of holistic healing. Nature and the body have a wisdom that should be listened to; mankind should not immediately rush in with medical interference for every problem."—*They Conquered AIDS! True Life Adventures,* by Scott J. Gregory and Bianca Leonardo.

We can help nature heal the body with correct, nutritious diet. "Let thy food be thy medicine," counselled Hippocrates. He used herbs, not drugs. Today, food supplements can help give vitally needed, nutritious elements to the body. Other natural elements the body needs are: fresh air, sunshine, water (internally and externally), exercise, sleep and rest, and the mental/spiritual elements, including prayer, meditation, positive thinking, cheerfulness, etc. These are the basic "7 Essentials of Health." There are sub-divisions, such as fasting, colon cleansing, etc.

The broadest definition of "medicine" is "The art and science of preventing and curing disease." (Webster's International Dictionary, Second Edition, Unabridged.)

"Holism" is defined as "the theory that reality is founded upon organic or unified wholes; emphasis on the importance of the whole and the interdependence of its parts." In holistic medicine, the mind is considered. Also, rather than treating parts of the body separately and materialistically as orthodox medicine does, the body is treated as a whole.

The author and publisher *do not include chemical medicine* in their use of the term "holistic." This book provides a holistic protocol (a system of treatment).

This editor, as founder/president of a vegetarian society for fifteen years, learned much about diet. She lectured and wrote about the vegetarian diet as the best diet. The *vegan* diet (no animal by-products) is even better; it is the purest and most natural diet available. More and more it is being realized that natural nutrition has a great deal to do with good health; conversely, a poor diet helps cause poor health. "We are what we eat."

"The New Medicine" is the new frontier in health. Here is the vital work for this last decade of this century—and beyond the year 2000.

Bianca Leonardo
Editor/Publisher

IMMUNO-SUPPRESSED?

This book was written primarily for doctors and patients who are receptive and willing to act on these new principles.

It is of the utmost importance that those individuals who need it the most — people who are immuno-suppressed — receive this protocol.

To date, *effective* treatment programs for conditions of immune suppression have not been developed. Some reasons are:

(1) Knowledge of the immune system is relatively new; the subject is vast.

(2) There is no one simple cure (such as a vaccine) for these conditions, because immune suppression involves the entire body— the blood which courses through all the cells, the glands (exocrine and endocrine) and the organs. Of course, there is also the mind— and its unlimited, and largely undiscovered, power.

(3) Most research being done is in allopathic (orthodox) medicine. Huge capital is required for research today, and only the federal government and the billion-dollar drug companies can undertake it. Private companies and the government have not invested funds in alternative therapy research. Alternative therapies, often more effective than toxic drugs, are by-passed by the federal Food and Drug Administration.

(4) Drugs do not cure immuno-suppressive diseases.

Causes of Immuno-Suppression

Millions of individuals today are immuno-suppressed. This can result in opportunistic infections. What are the causes of immuno-suppression?

Most certainly, some causes are devitalized foods, our polluted environment, the stress of living in cities, stress in relationships, drugs, alcohol, tobacco, and other harmful substances that are used. Drugs (legal and illegal) are significant causes.

Is it not possible that children who continually get colds, the flu, are often sick, constantly being vaccinated—are immuno-suppressed, although not so called? These children become adults, and carry with them a weakened immune system.

Opportunistic infections do not come without a cause. Immunity starts with a healthy mother (and, it is said, from mother's milk for the newborn and until weaning). Also from a healthy father, and from prenatal and childhood factors.

The conditions that cause immuno-suppression are cumulative. Diseases of immuno-suppression do not come "like a thief in the night," or from sudden attacks of viruses or microbes. These diseases have deep-seated causes. Viruses appear in a compromised immune system.

Today, we really do not know why one person becomes HIV-Positive and another does not. One member of a family may develop Candida; another will not. Why?

Although there may be predisposing factors beyond the control of the patient, yet it is our conviction that these conditions are largely brought on by what people do to themselves and allow others to do to them.

In this protocol, therapies alternative to allopathy are used. Of course, the patient must cooperate with and have faith in the treatment.

The author has been researching immuno-suppression since 1980. Some individuals (his patients and others) have reversed AIDS and other conditions, using "The New Medicine."

For consultation (in person or via telephone), call (310) 459-2680

Call 213-960-7999 to leave a message.

Scott J. Gregory, O. M. D., Author.

Note: Some of the products described in this book require monitoring by a health care practitioner. Therefore, sources for all products are not given. Some sources are listed on page 85.

General Treatment Principles
and
Protocol for the Immune System

   I.   Utilization of non-toxic germicides to eliminate the pathogens

   II. Detoxification to rid the body of metabolic wastes

   III. Increasing cellular metabolism to energize the body

   IV. Cellular repair to rebuild the immune system

The Four Categories Explained

The four protocol categories are listed as I, II, III, and IV. Specific supplements are described for each group. Following this, there are treatments for each opportunistic infection.

The primary approach of: (1) killing the virus; (2) detoxifying metabolic wastes; (3) energizing the body; (4) cellular repair — is sequential (following a specific order), and is valid *in most cases.*

In certain cases, it is important that the highly urgent symptoms be addressed first. For example, if a patient has diarrhea, flu-like symptoms, fever, etc., those conditions need attention urgently.

It is counter-productive to stimulate diseased T-cells, white blood cells, and interferon at too early a stage, without getting rid of the viruses first; this could spread more infection.

The Time Frame of Treatment

Each phase of treatment, (category), choosing from among the supplements listed and other therapies described, lasts approximately four to six weeks. In 16 to 24 weeks, one could possibly be free from all symptoms and conditions. Some patients stop treatment too soon; others get discouraged.

Product Usage and Availability

There are many products listed in each of the four categories. The author is not recommending that *all* be used. The reader should not feel overwhelmed by the number of supplements described. It is always best to have the guidance of a qualified health care professional familiar with this protocol.

The author has researched these products, and the ones included seem to be most efficacious. Many of the supplements are widely available from health food stores, supplement mail order companies, and naturopathic pharmacies.

A few of the products are "protected"—sold only through health practitioners. If the reader cannot locate a product, he may telephone the author.

Intuition Important

With the assistance of a holistic health practitioner and some intuition, an individual might choose those products he has a proclivity for and that suit his needs. The patient should be an active participant in his healing process, and that is one of the reasons this book was written. If the patient has used natural medicine, he has some experience with it and can ascertain, to a certain extent, what works best for his body—be it homeopathy, Chinese herbs, etc. However, the rule in treatment is: "Do not treat yourself without guidance."

1

Detailed Descriptions of Protocol

I. UTILIZATION OF NON-TOXIC GERMICIDES

Herbal Tonic
Pfaffia Paniculata
LDM-100
PDL-500
Mycocyde I and II
Phellostatin
Can-Di-Gest

H-II-L (Herpezyme II)
Dioxychlor
Hydrogen Peroxide
Bacillus Laterosporus
Monolaurin
Capricin
Butyrate Plus

Garlic Plus
Echinacea
Isatis 6
Composition A
Golden Seal
Pau d'Arco; (Taheebo Tea) *
Aloe-Ace™ **

* Description found in Section II.
** Description found in Section IV.

Herbal Tonic

A tonic that contains ten U. S. Indian herbs that stain abnormal cells, causing them to die. The Herbal Tonic:

(1) Destroys pathogenic viruses, bacteria, fungi, and parasites by disrupting their cell membranes and their replication.

(2) Oxygenates the mitochondria (the energy-producing components of cells).

(3) Migrates past the blood-brain barrier, to destroy pathogens residing there.

(4) Increases the immune response.

(5) Stabilizes the body weight; increases appetite in a convalescing patient.

(6) Expels potentially dangerous toxins.

(7) Is complementary; can be used with any other holistic treatment and type of supplementation (except aloe vera).

(8) Due to its high mineral content, promotes better functioning of the organs, and nourishes them. Nourishes the blood, making the cells healthier.

(9) Diluted, can be used topically for lesions and sores.

(10) Herbal Tonic has a multitude of uses, with many kinds of degenerative diseases. We have classified this tonic as a germicide, but it can fit into any of the categories: I, II, III, or IV.

(11) It is a nutritional adjunct to the diet.

(12) The extract has no restricted shelf life. It does not deteriorate or lose its potency, and is not affected by heat or cold.

Herbal Tonic can improve everyone's health.

Suggested dosage: one drop three times a day, with meals or immediately thereafter. (Can cause nausea if taken on an empty stomach.) After two days, use two drops. After two or three days, increase one drop. Go up to six drops. If a person can increase to six drops without nausea, he should. Increase to whatever you can tolerate, slowly; twenty drops, maximum.

There are no side effects from this product, but one may go through a detoxification phase. If so, lower the dosage. Usually, after three weeks, symptoms have vanished. One needs to stay on it. For serious conditions, such as Epstein-Barr, Herpes, Candida, etc. three or more months are required with Herbal Tonic at the maximum dose, then going to a maintenance dose, depending on the severity of the condition.

It is precious and special, so the patient must be willing to continue the use of Herbal Tonic.

Topical application: one to three drops in two to four ounces of distilled water. Herbal Tonic may be put on food, taken in beverages, or may be capsulized and taken in that form. One may gargle with dilute solutions.

Source: The author makes it available to his patients.

Pfaffia Paniculata

Pfaffia (fă' fē ă) Paniculata is one of the most exciting new herbs. It has a wide range of efficacy for chronic diseases, with documented case histories. Reported improvement has been substantiated in clinical cases of:

- Bone joint illnesses
- Bone sarcomas
- Candidiasis
- Carcinomas
- Control of cholesterol (particularly of HDL)
- Diabetes
- Estrogen imbalance
- Lymphomas
- Osteomyelitis
- Urea control (uric acid)

From deep in the rain forests of Brazil comes *Pfaffia Paniculata*. Its use among the natives is widespread, and has been so for centuries. Here is their most revered plant which the Indians call "the one that cures all things." They describe it as a source of energy and a rejuvenator; also a treatment for the most serious diseases. It is a food, not a chemical, and the entire plant is used—the root, stems, and branches. It is a well-balanced energizer, which supports the body's immune system. It is known world-wide as an adaptogen. Natives shared it with a famous Brazilian botanist in 1975—making it available to the modern world.

It is particularly indicated for conditions attended by low energy, coldness, pallor, weak digestion, lack of spirit and libido. Such diseases as Epstein-Barr, Hodgkin's Disease, Leukemia, Multiple Sclerosis, and Diabetes may be significantly improved by the use of Pfaffia on a regular basis.

Specifically, Pfaffia is used for Chronic Fatigue and Exhaustion, diseases in which conditions are that of cold, weakness, and lack of energy. It is not recommended for inflammatory conditions. There is no toxicity. According to traditional Chinese Medicine, it is indicated for a spleen-yang condition (pale tongue and weak pulse), and serves as a Chi tonic. It is also used for menopause conditions and heart and circulatory disorders. A very safe and effective herb to use.

LDM-100

LDM-100, a plant antibiotic, is an extract of the wild black carrot. This plant was used as a food and a medicine by the Indians of the Northwest. It was one of the best known and most widely used remedies. The root of the plant was most commonly used to treat coughs, colds, hay fever, bronchitis, asthma, influenza, pneumonia, tuberculosis, etc.

This product was introduced into Western medicine by the famous medical doctor, E. T. Krebs, Sr., of the Vitamin B-15 and Vitamin B-17 fame. It is gaining world-wide recognition. E. T. Krebs, Jr. once made the statement concerning the virtues of this wonderful natural herb, that "it is destined to become one of the most important antibiotic herbs known to man."

The crude oil of the plant and a concentration of 1:10 in mineral oil completely or partially inhibited growth of ten organisms, including all gram positive ones. A study of the effectiveness of extracts prepared from the root of *Lomatia dissectum* showed varying degrees of inhibition of the growth of all 62 strains and species of bacteria and fungi tested (Carlson, 1948). There are many other antibiotic studies of this plant. Historically, it is one of the most important medicinal plants of the western United States, and has great potential as a modern therapeutic agent.

LDM-100 is very alkaline and makes the saliva and urine alkaline.

The saliva pH pattern averages about 6.6, while the urine pH pattern averages about 5.6. Urine pH below 6.9 suggests possible infection. LDM-100 creates an alkaline environment (demonstrated in the saliva and the urine) which kills acid-fast bacteria and viruses. Any reading below 7 is acid; a reading above 7 is alkaline. A patient can chart his recovery by testing his saliva and urine. The more alkaline the state, the less infection.

Viral Infections: Used for Epstein-Barr Virus, Herpes, Colds, Influenza, Trachoma, Lansing Polio Virus, Meningitis, etc.

Bacterial Infections: Lymes Disease, Pneumonia, Urinary and Pulmonary Infections; Staphylococcus and Streptococcus Infections.

Fungus Infections: Candida Albicans, Intestinal Infections, Athlete's Foot, Finger and Toenail Infections.

Contraindications: LDM-100 has essential oils which produce a harmless skin rash. It is a sign that one's immune system has been stimulated. This is counter-irritant therapy and is beneficial for the immune system. The rash lasts only a few days, and is not harmful.

Botanical Source: *Leptotaenia dissecta*

Form: This product comes packed in 30 ml (1 oz.) amber dropper bottles.

LDM-100 is composed of a single herbal extract *(Leptotaenia dissecta* var. *multifida)* employing a special processing technique. It is virustatic, fungicidal and bacteriocidal/bacteriostatic. This non-toxic antibiotic extract is one of the most important infection fighters in existence.

LDM-100 is extremely effective because of the presence of immune-stimulating polysaccharides. (Study by Wakeman, 1925.)

LDM-100 has anti-viral, anti-fungal and anti-microbial activity, according to investigations. LDM-100 easily permeates the virus coat as well as bacterial, yeast, and animal cells, demonstrated *in vitro* (in the test tube) and *in vivo* (in the body).

Dosage : No toxicity levels. First 4 days usage: 1/2 dropperful 4 times a day. Second 4 days: after rotation, 1/2 dropperful twice a day. It may be taken directly with the dropper, or put into water or juice.

PDL-500

PDL-500 is a virucide, specifically for HIV, AIDS, and ARC. It contains the same herbs as LDM-100, plus some herbs from the Yucatan Peninsula.

The dosage is the same as that for LDM-100, and it is used in a rotation of 4 days on and 4 days off.

Some highly sensitive people may develop a skin rash on the arms and legs, lasting a few days.

Mycocyde I and II

Mycocyde I and II are anti-Candidiasis formulas. These products are indicated for general yeast infections, Candidiasis and Candida Albicans. Formula I contains Echinacea, which acts in ways as a lymphogogue, tonifying the lymph system, preparing the body for the action of Formula II. Formula I helps in building the immune system, stimulating cells to produce interferon. Special extracting techniques for this tincture pull all the active medicinal substances from the plants, so they can be utilized by the body.

Formula II contains specifically designed herbs which act synergistically to combat Candida infections.

The product comes in 60 ml. (2-oz.) amber dropper bottles.

Dosage: Formula I is taken first; a half hour later, one takes Formula II. Amount: 1/2 dropperful, in each case, 4 times daily.

That is the first rotation. On the second, reduce the frequency to twice a day. A rotation consists of four days. After that, you move on to another anti-viral.

Phellostatin

Phellostatin is a broad spectrum anti-fungal derived from Chinese herbs, specifically 12 herbs. The company name is Chinese Traditional Formulas. Used specifically for Candidiasis, this product will cause a rapid die-off of the Candidiasis fungus, and is a powerful anti-fungal formula. It stimulates the immune system and resolves heat in the lower part of the body (stomach, genitalia). These are Chinese herbs that help to correct spleen-yang deficiency.

Dosage: 3 tablets before each meal. Non-toxic.

Can-Di-Gest

Can-Di-Gest is a unique strain of a specialized hypo-allergenic bio-culture, imported from Japan. This potent but friendly gastro-intestinal super-culture is *Lacto-bacillus salivarious*, which is normally present in the digestive tract of man.

Can-Di-Gest increases energy because food is more readily utilized. Ammonia chains are broken down so as not to be harmful. It purifies the entire colon, repairs the intestinal tract, and boosts the brain function.

Can-Di-Gest improves the ecological balance in your body. There are no binders or fillers in this product. Lactose-intolerant individuals were able to digest dairy products after using Can-Di-Gest. Food-sensitive individuals should start with very low doses— one or less capsule per day.

Normal, suggested **dosage:** Take 1 to 4 capsules with cool water, once or twice a day. Again, this product is very potent, and can cause mild constipation, so it is best to start on a low dosage and work up.

H-II-L (Herpezyme II)

This product is a liquid, herbal tincture, specifically manufactured for Herpes II. It can be applied topically and also taken internally, when there is an outbreak. As mentioned in the Herpes section, the best way to attack Herpes is when it is in its active state. Otherwise, it lies dormant in the dorsal nerve root of the spine. This product can exacerbate an outbreak, and this is a good sign, because when it is active, it can be treated.

Dosage: same dosage as LDM-100 and PDL-500—1/2 dropperful 4 times a day for the first 4 days. On the second rotation, 1/2 dropperful twice a day.

Dioxychlor

Dr. Robert Bradford and Dr. Rodrigo Rodriguez, M.D. of the American Biologics-Mexico SA Research Hospital, a medical center in Tijuana, B.C., Mexico, have done research on immuno-suppression, diet modification and organism environmental control.

Their research has shown that Dioxychlor compounds that liberate nascent (atomic) oxygen inhibit spores, mycoplasmas, viruses and fungi. They have done studies *in vitro* and *in vivo*. It has been found to kill yeast cells in the body. There are no side effects (as there are with Nystatin).

Nystatin is a prescription drug used to suppress Candidiasis. As with all other drugs, sensitivity from its use develops in some individuals. With continued use, a plateau is reached. Often, with drugs, smaller dosages are no longer effective; stronger doses cause toxicity, with serious reactions as the result.

Dioxychlor kills pathogenic microbes on contact, and it has been proven at the Bradford Institute to be a powerful inorganic substance effective against Candida Albicans.

The nascent oxygen released by using Dioxychlor is stored in the body. Dioxychlor is not new; it was used in World War I for infections. Stanford University has done much research on it.

When Dioxychlor is taken homeopathically under the tongue, it goes directly into the lymph system, as opposed to diluting it and taking it in water. Individuals who have chemical sensitivities must start out with very low dosages sublingually. (4-5 drops is the manufacturer's suggestion.)

Dosage: 14 to 16 drops for 4 days in 2 ounces of water.

Dioxychlor is available only through health care professionals.

Hydrogen Peroxide (H$_2$O$_2$)

Hydrogen Peroxide is a common substance with "magical" powers, whose significance is unknown or neglected by medical doctors. There are over four thousand research papers today on hydrogen peroxide. Much of this research has been done at the Mayo Clinic. Yet, you will not find hydrogen peroxide mentioned in the Medical Desk Reference.

Hydrogen Peroxide is water plus another part of oxygen (H$_2$O$_2$). It bubbles with oxygen, is antiseptic and kills germs.

In a healthy condition, the body produces hydrogen peroxide as part of the immune system. H$_2$O$_2$ is produced by the white blood cells. It is the first line of defense.

We live in an ocean of micro-organisms, each one seeking out its own little habitat in our bodies — from the tops of our heads to the bottom of our toes. We can control or eliminate them from our bodies by drinking a simple solution of hydrogen peroxide!

McGraw Hill's *Encyclopedia of Science*, Fifth Edition, states that hydrogen peroxide exists in rain and snow, mountains and streams. How does it get there? It gets there from the ozone layer. Sunlight and the ultraviolet rays split the O_2 molecule. If not destroyed by pollution, the ozone reaches the ground. The hydrogen peroxide gets into our fruits and vegetables. It is a by-product of the photosynthesis process.

Hydrogen peroxide is not as unstable as believed. If you take a 3% solution of hydrogen peroxide and boil it, and check it for the liberation of O_2, the O_2 will still be present. It is not easily destroyed.

Human mother's milk, and especially colostrum, the "first milk," contains a high percentage of hydrogen peroxide; that could possibly be where we get our immunity. But how many babies are breast fed? Ever since commercial formulas were developed, and pushed on new mothers in the hospitals, very few (although there is a new trend among some young mothers to return to breast feeding).

Lancet, the renowned British medical journal, states that hydrogen peroxide has been used successfully with malaria patients. It has been used in many other ways, also — as an oxygen source at Cape Canaveral for the astronauts; as a preservative in products (food grade) — it triples the shelf life of many foods; aloe vera gel has naturally occurring hydrogen peroxide, and is used to heal wounds and burns.

In Europe, hydrogen peroxide is added to drinking water to purify it, instead of the chlorine and ammonia we use, because it has 5,000 times more killing power on bacteria than chlorine and ammonia. So why do we not use it, too?

At Lourdes, France, the water was tested and found to contain hydrogen peroxide and germanium. So — it is more than people's faith that is curing them at Lourdes!

The T-lymphocytes engulf and secrete chemicals that kill foreign cells. Two very important substances — hydrogen peroxide and superoxide dismutase — are both reactive forms of oxygen. These materials are lethal to foreign bodies. AIDS is caused by a pathogen that cannot survive more than five minutes outside the body. Why? The germ is anaerobic: it cannot live in a high-oxygen environment. When hydrogen peroxide is taken into the body, it raises the oxygen level, oxygenates the cells, and kills viruses.

Dr. George Sperti, a medical researcher, is connected with the St. Thomas Institute in Cincinnati, Ohio. He has over 23 patents, including two called Preparation H and Asper gum. For 14 months in the Cincinnati, Ohio Cancer Center, he conducted experiments on cancerous mice. **In 30 to 60 days, 90% recovered, when treated with hydrogen peroxide in their drinking water. The tumors went into remission!**

When hydrogen peroxide is put into the system, it enters the bloodstream; there it seeks out the micro-organisms and destroys them.

Scientists at the University of Iowa, University of Wisconsin, and Wabash College, Crawfordsville, Indiana, hypothesized that hydrogen peroxide is the ultimate cause of normal cell division.

We believe that a deficiency of hydrogen peroxide production increases an individual's susceptibility to infection.

Micro-organisms themselves possess an electrical charge. When one suspends these organisms in an aqueous solution on an electrical plate, they will gravitate toward the positive charge. The hydrogen peroxide is missing an electron on its outer orbit, and will accept an electron to complete its outer orbit. The result of electrons being taken away from micro-organisms is dead matter.

Hydrogen peroxide taken orally has been researched by Dr. Edward Carl Rosenow of the Mayo Clinic. Pathogens invade, attack cells, building cocoons around the stricken cells, cutting off blood supply and nutrition, causing only the infected cells to live, as in cancer and AIDS. O_2 increases the elimination of toxins. O_1 in ozone or hydrogen peroxide kills the infection.

Hydrogen peroxide, taken internally, must be without preservatives or stabilizers.

Dr. Otto Warburg (twice a Nobel laureate), states that "Cancer cannot live in a high oxygen environment."

Dr. Rosenow took germ cells and fed them different foods and put them in a different environment; he got a different disease. When the food and environments were changed back to the original, the original disease resulted.

Conclusion: specific germs live and multiply in specific environments. If the environment is changed, the germ will either leave or be destroyed.

Internal Use

Use 35% Food Grade, and **always dilute with water.**

Most important with using H_2O_2 internally is proper dilution and proper dosage schedules. Use it no more than four days at a time.

Dosage: The first day: 3 drops of 35% Food Grade in at least 4 ounces of water, prune juice, apple juice, or orange juice. (Fruit juices mask the taste.)

Each additional day, you increase one drop. When you get up to 26 drops, you maintain that for 4 days. Then rotate to the other anti-virals. H_2O_2 is best taken on an empty stomach in the morning or at bedtime.

Bio-Oxidation Therapy— External Use

Bio-Oxidation has been done in the past via infusions or intravenously (running H_2O_2 through the veins). The new protocol suggests it be applied topically. This is cost effective, painless, and the patient can do it himself.

H_2O_2 affects the internal and external simultaneously. While being applied topically, it is also absorbed by the cells.

Hydrogen peroxide is used for opportunistic infections as well as for skin rashes, brought on by such infections.

For rashes, use 3% hydrogen peroxide. This solution can be purchased at your local drug store. Put into a plastic mister spray bottle, and spray the body from the neck down in the shower; rub into the skin. Treat yourself once a day.

As the H_2O_2 soaks into the skin, there will be a slight stinging sensation that will last about seven minutes and then vanish. This is caused by nascent oxygen being absorbed into your body.

Each tablespoon of 3% hydrogen peroxide provides you with the equivalent of 22 drops of 35% hydrogen peroxide. In other words, the H_2O_2 is absorbed into your system through the skin. In severe cases, the topical spray may be applied two or three times a day, and it will foam up in areas where the bacteria are present. It should also be sprayed into the oral cavity or gargled, and sprayed in the groin, the rectum, and any other place where infection is present. Candidiasis in the mouth is called thrush; many AIDS/ARC patients have it.

To spread, a virus must travel. Every cell is immersed in body fluids, mostly the intercellular fluid. If the intercellular fluids have all the oxygen compounds, enzymes, peroxides, minerals, electrolysis processes and compounds, etc. that they need, as in an optimum health situation, then the virus might have a hard time leaving its host cell and moving out to infect other cells.

Bacillus Laterosporus, BOD Strain—Flora-Balance™

Restores and corrects bacterial balance

One of the most important steps in therapy for Candidiasis and other immuno-suppressive conditions is to restore normal bacterial flora. Failure to replace healthy flora will lead to a relapse, no matter what means are taken to kill the yeast cells. Bacillus Laterosporus, BOD strain, sold under the name of Flora-Balance*, is available in a liquid form (16 ounces, 1-month average supply), or bottles of 60 capsules (2-month supply). It has a 1 to 2 year shelf life and needs no refrigeration. The product is recommended when antibiotics have been used. Usage should be monitored by a health professional.

Dosage: Liquid, 2 tablespoons in 2 oz. of distilled water on an empty stomach 20 minutes before eating, once daily. After 1 month, dosage may be reduced to 1 tablespoon with 1 ounce of water daily.

Capsules: First month, 2 capsules daily, 20 minutes or more before eating. Thereafter, 1 capsule daily. Capsules are more convenient, and last twice as long as the liquid, per bottle, at the same price.

Some people may not tolerate these doses and may need to gradually work up to recommended amounts.

A scientist describes Bacillus Laterosporus as a live organism which punctures the cell membrane of bacteria and fungi, consuming them "phagocytically" (eating and digesting).

Flora-Balance liquid, or capsules emptied into warm water, may be used as a gargle for thrush, or vaginally in a 1-1 ratio with 2 ounces of water for local fungal infections. Apply for 20 minutes.

Bacillus Laterosporus, BOD Strain—Topical Uses

Flora-Balance liquid or dissolved capsules may also be applied topically to fungal growths on the body, such as nail or scalp fungus. Allow 20-30 minutes daily application to affected areas.

---

*For the public, and Latero-Flora™ for health professionals.

Monolaurin

Viral and fungal diseases result from a series of growth cycles that kill or alter the cells. The maximum goal of anti-viral treatment is to restore the function to the infected cell without harming the body's cells. Most of the substances that do this are toxic or have serious side effects, and have not gained broad acceptance in the medical community. Consequently, there is a void in treatment procedures.

An alternative solution is to use a class of safe substances which are fatty acids and glycerol esters. Fatty acids have been used as germicides for centuries; glycerol esters (derivatives of fatty acids) are a recent addition. Because of their lack of toxicity and known biochemical pathways, glycerol esters have been shown to be more effective than their corresponding fatty acids.

One of these esters, Monolaurin (Lauricidin), has recently been selected for extensive studies at medical research centers because of its high anti-microbial activity. In studies performed at the Respiratory Virology Branch, Centers for Disease Control, Atlanta, Georgia, Monolaurin was tested for virucidal activity against 14 human RNA and DNA enveloped viruses in cell culture. Monolaurin removed all measurable infectivity by disintegrating the virus envelope.

Each of the Monolaurin samples effected a >99.9% killing of the 14 viruses tested in the CDC study.

Monolaurin is a monoglycerol ester of the fatty acid laurate. Laurate fatty acids contain twelve carbon atoms, are present in many animals and plants and have been shown to possess wide-spectrum activity against fungi and viruses. Lauric acid is present in human milk, amniotic fluid, adipose tissues, urine, cow's milk, butter, spermaceti, palm kernel oil and coconut oil.

Dosage: *Monolaurin must be taken on an empty stomach.* Take six capsules per day. The best times are 7:00 to 8:00 A.M., 3:00 to 4:00 P.M., and 9:00 to 10:00 P.M. After taking Monolaurin, wait at least one hour before eating any food. Monolaurin may be used together with the above anti-virals. However, Monolaurin is not taken in a rotation sequence. It can be used continuously for 30 days.

Capricin

Capricin is a time-released fungicide. It eliminates unfriendly fungi without destroying the patient's friendly flora. It is important to note that the Candida Albicans fungus is able to penetrate deep into the convolutions of the intestinal tract. Capricin, being a lipid solution, is able to penetrate the cellular membrane, eliminating both the surface and inter-cellular Candida.

Dosage: 12 capsules per day *with meals*. Take for about one month. It works better when taken with Butyrate Plus.

Capricin contains caprylic acid from coconut oil which kills Candida Albicans in the intestinal tract.

Butyrate Plus
(Multi-Nutrient Butyrate)

This product contains butyric acid, magnesium and calcium in a special proportion. Also contains Vitamin A (palmitate), Beta Carotene and Pantothenic Acid.

(1) Butyrate Plus is suitable for Candidiasis because it helps the body to produce short-chain fatty acids. A person who has Candidiasis may lose a considerable amount of weight, due to the malabsorption syndrome.

(2) It will benefit most food allergies and food sensitivities.

(3) Butyric acid is extremely healing to the gastro-mucosa (large and small intestines, stomach). Butyrates repair the damage from the bacteria. The Candida bacteria bore holes in the intestine, and that is one of the reasons for leakage of foreign substances into the bloodstream.

(4) It boosts the immune function by detoxifying the lymph system.

(5) Butyrate Plus is free from corn, wheat, dairy, yeast, sugar, salt, starch, and artificial colors.

Dosage: This product must be taken with food for it to work. Follow directions on the label.

Garlic Plus

Garlic Plus contains garlic, Germanium, and Chlorophyllium. It should be used with Capricin and Butyrate Plus. All must be taken with food.

Dosage: same as that of Capricin and Butyrate Plus. See general manufacturer's directions for specific doses.

Garlic has been used throughout the centuries because of its anti-viral properties. Its chemical configuration is extremely complicated. It is very high in B vitamins, specifically thiamine. It contains germanium, which is an interferon producer. It has anti-bacterial and anti-fungal properties. It is especially advantageous because it is safe, non-toxic, and doesn't cause other health problems. There is, of course, the odor problem. Some of the active ingredients have been removed from the deodorized garlic.

The second problem with garlic is that it contains large quantities of sodium.

Echinacea

This native American herb is used for blood purification, including the stimulation of vital organs. It neutralizes acids, removes excess fat where toxins are retained, **is effective as a natural antibiotic and inhibits growth of bacteria, viruses and parasites.** It can be made into a tea.

The Echinacea made by Cardiovascular Research is most effective. All three different plant types are included in this product: Echinacea Augustifolia, Echinacea Pallida, Echinacea Purpurea.

Isatis 6

Isatis 6 consists of six Chinese herbs that are anti-viral in nature, which target toxins in the blood and resolve heat conditions. The Chinese formula is Da Qing Jie Du Pian. The ingredients are: isatis, hu-chang, prunella, oldenlandia, andrographis, lonicera.

It is the author's conviction that in certain situations, Chinese herbs can alleviate conditions and benefit the individual when all else proves inadequate.

Composition "A"

Composition "A" is a synergistically prepared herbal formula specifically designed for HIV infection. It works three ways:

(1) It resolves toxic elements in the blood.

(2) It addresses the HIV virus with specific Chinese anti-viral herbs (over 15).

(3) It rebuilds the body's ability to fight off pathogenic infections.

In the protocol, use only for HIV (not for KS lesions). Nevertheless, when this product is combined with Zendoria formula, it is very effective.

Dosage: See suggested dosage by manufacturer. No toxicity.

Thyme

Many cases of scalp itching and flaking, other than Seborrhea, can be Candidiasis. These can be treated with the spice thyme. Make an herbal infusion and rub it into the scalp, upon arising or at bedtime.

B.F.I. Antiseptic Powder

(Totally external use)

You can buy this item in your drug store. Rub into the skin. It stops itching and is good for rashes or athlete's foot. It promotes healing, especially on fungus infections of the feet and dermatitis. Do not apply to raw skin, wounds or burns.

Ingredients: Bismuth-Formic-Iodide, Amol, Bismuth Subgallate, Boric Acid, Eucalyptol, Menthol, Potassium Alum, Thymol, Zinc Phenolsulfonate.

Golden Seal

Golden Seal powder is used externally for infection and also internally. It acts to invigorate and strengthen the body with great antiseptic qualities; it kills poisons very effectively. It can be made into a tea — 1 teaspoon in boiling water. (Can take up to two cups per day.) It can also be applied topically as a powder or wet as a poultice. If taken over a long period of time, it can cause low blood sugar.

Bee Kind

Bee Kind is the first natural suppository style douche. It has been used successfully where conditions such as vaginitis, including candidiasis and cystitis, exist. It can also be used rectally.

This natural solution consists of honey, aloe vera, myrrh and yarrow.

Honey has been used since ancient times for its wound-healing and antiseptic properties. At least 2,000 papers and articles have been published in scientific and medical journals and elsewhere describing the beneficial, biological effects of honey. In one study, it was reported that when 100% undiluted honey was applied to wounds, no pathogens (including Candida Albicans) grew and in fact were destroyed. Honey was found to be much more effective than the expensive topical antibiotics that had previously been used.

Honey, aloe vera, myrrh and yarrow collectively are recognized and reported to have the following properties and effects: stimulation of cell regeneration, astringent and emollient qualities, antibacterial, antiseptic, antimicrobial, antifungal, disinfectant, aromatic, cleansing, soothing and healing (especially soothing to mucous membranes).

Research on the anti-inflammation, antibacterial and antifungal properties of honey and aloe vera show why BEE KIND works well where irritation and infection are present, with myrrh and yarrow contributing similar and additional properties.

Over 181 substances are known to be present in honey alone. Altogether, the substances found in honey, aloe, myrrh and yarrow include simple and complex carbohydrates, enzymes, minerals, low levels of vitamins, trace elements, aroma constituents, proteins and amino acids.

Included in the numerous beneficial constituents, of note are: caprylic, lauric and butyric acids, oleic and linoleic acids, lactic, citric and glutamic acids, tannins, flavonoids, saponins, sulfur, hydrogen peroxide (trace amounts in honey), lysine and magnesium.

This formula may possibly aid in replenishing a depleted magnesium supply in the vagina, as honey and aloe vera contain high levels of magnesium.

(See Page 85 for source)

SUMMARY OF GERMICIDES AND THEIR USES

For General Conditions

Name	Function	Description	Dosage	Contraindications
Herbal Tonic	Virucide, bactericide, fungicide parasiticide	A concentrated extract, containing ten U.S. Indian herbs, trace elements and minerals, such as : zinc, potassium, barium, iron, sodium, calcium, copper, etc.	Dilute two to three drops in four or more ounces of water.	Must be taken with food or nausea will result. Should be monitored by a health care practitioner, so that detoxification does not occur too quickly.
Pfaffia Paniculata	Powerful adaptogen* virucide, bactericide, fungicide.	An herb from the Amazonian rain forest. Used for a wide range of chronic diseases, specifically Epstein-Barr (weakness and fatigue).	Large dosages required; 8-12 capsules 3 times a day (up to 36 capsules per day).	Not effective for inflammatory conditions, fevers. Not to be used during pregnancy.
LDM-100 Lomatia dissectum (Liquid)	Virucide, bactericide, fungicide	A plant antibiotic from the wild black carrot root. For colds, influenza, Candidiasis, Herpes I and II, shingles, athlete's foot, pneumonia.	No toxicity levels. First 4 days usage: 1/2 dropperful 4 times a day. Second 4 days: after rotation, 1/2 dropperful twice a day. It may be taken directly with the dropper, or put into water or juice. Used in rotation 4 days on, and 4 days off.	Can cause a harmless, temporary skin rash.
Hydrogen Peroxide (H_2O_2) (Liquid)	Virucide, bactericide, fungicide	Natural-occurring compound, of hydrogen and oxygen. Found most abundantly in the body, also in rain, snow, etc. Helps make up our immune system.	See page 16 for dosage.	Strong oxidizing agent; can burn; do not exceed suggested dosages.
Aloe-Ace ™	Anti-inflammatory, antiseptic, anti-viral	The sap, rind and gel of the Aloe Vera plant (organically grown). The entire leaf of the plant is used, including acemannan.	For internal use, 1/2 capful in 8 ounces of one's favorite juice or water, twice a day, either on an empty stomach or with meals. For more severe infections, 1 - 1 1/2 capfuls 3 times a day is suggested.. Use in rotation, 4 days on, 4 days off.	No toxic side effects.

* Adaptogen—Restores balance and harmony in the body, without any side effects. Adaptogens enhance endurance and augment vitality.

For General Conditions

Name	Function	Description	Dosage	Contraindications
Dioxychlor (Liquid)	Virucide, fungicide, bactericide	Inorganic substance, non-toxic	Used in rotation, 4 days on, 4 days off. Can be taken homeopathically under the tongue, 4-5 drops, or can be diluted in water (12-25 drops in 6-8 ounces of water).	Chemically-sensitive persons should use low dosages.

For Specific Conditions

Name	Function	Description	Dosage	Contraindications
PDL-500 (Liquid)	Virucide	An herbal tincture from the Yucatan. Used in place of LDM-100, specifically in cases of HIV Infection, ARC/AIDS	Same as LDM-100, used in rotation (4 days on, 4 days off).	Same contraindication as LDM-100.
Mycocyde I and II	Fungicide for general yeast infection and skin fungus.	For Candidiasis. Plant sources: Echinacea augustifolia; Cayenne; Fern Bush; Desert Globe Mallow	Same as LDM-100 and PDL-500.	Can cause temporary rash on arms and legs.
Phellostatin	Fungicide and immune stimulant	For Candidiasis. Six Chinese herbs that astringe heat in the lower part of body (stomach, genitals).	Three tablets before each meal.	None
Can-Di-Gest (Super *Lactobacillus Salivarious*)	Fungicide, bactericide, virucide	Naturally occurs in the digestive tract. Very potent. Destroys pathogenic bacteria and fungi in the digestive tract. Detoxifies the lymph system. Breaks down and digests organic matter. 100% pure, no binders or fillers. It engulfs uric acid in the body. A brain stimulant. For Candidiasis and malabsorption syndrome.	Take carefully. Start with 1-4 capsules, with cool water once or twice a day. Capsules may be dissolved in mouth or throat, or can be taken vaginally. May be taken by milk-sensitive individuals, who should start with 1/8 of a capsule.	This product needs to be initiated slowly; otherwise, it may cause constipation/diarrhea/bloating. These conditions are temporary; the microbes are dying off. Needs to be refrigerated.
H-II-L (Herpezyme II) (For Herpes Type II)	Virucide	Total plant source (contains LDM-100 plus herbs Andean Borage and Leptotaenia).	Same as LDM-100 and PDL-500 and Mycocyde. May be applied topically to Herpes lesions.	May cause slight, temporary rash.

22 •

For Specific Conditions

Name	Function	Description	Dosage	Contraindications
Bacillus Laterosporus (Flora-Balance/Latero-Flora) (Liquid or Capsules)	Bactericide, fungicide, virucide	Non-lacto bacillus bacteria. A living organism that punctures pathogenic cell membranes and digests them.	*Liquid:* 1 to 2 TBs in 2 oz. water once daily. *Capsules:* 1 to 2 capsules once daily. Always on an empty stomach, 20 mins. before meals. Can be rotated.	Some individuals may not tolerate this dosage. May be reduced, gradually working up.
Monolaurin	Virucide, fungicide	A monoglycol ester of the fatty acid laurate	Six capsules total per day (two be-tween meals).	None
Capricin (Calcium Magnesium Caprylate)	Time-released fungicide	A lipid solution. Eliminates both surface and intestinal Candida. Contains caprylic acid from coconut oil.	See manufacturer's recommendation.	Can be hard on the liver with extended use.
Butyrate Plus (Multi-Nutrient Butyrate)	Fungicide and digestant (helps the body digest food). Short-chain fatty acids. Specifically for Candida and malabsorption syndrome.	For weight loss; repairs damage that Candida has done in the digestive tract; aids in the assimilation of foods.	This product and Capricin only work when taken with food. Take the two products together.	None
Garlic Plus	Anti-viral properties	Garlic Plus contains garlic, Germanium, and Chlorophyllium. Should be used together with Capricin and Butyrate Plus.	Follow manufacturer's recommendation	None
Isatis 6	The #1 anti-viral for pneumocystis, HIV, targeting viruses, bacteria, and viral infections. Use for a sore throat.	Contains six Chinese herbs.	2-3 tablets, 3 times a day, 1/2 hour before meals.	None
Composition "A"	Anti-pyrogenic (abolishes heat), anti-viral, anti-cancer	Synergistically prepared Chinese herbal formula, specifically for HIV infection, which targets the T-cells.	Manufacturer's suggestion	None
Echinacea	Bactericide, fungicide, vermicide (kills parasites and worms).	A native American herb that purifies blood, neutralizes acids, and removes toxins. A natural antibiotic.	One teaspoon steeped in boiled, distilled water. In tablet form, 2 cap-sules per day.	In small quantities, there are no problems.
Golden Seal	Bactericide, antiseptic. For internal and external use: good on open sores.	Tonic, laxative, a healing herb. Aids appetite and digestion. Good for Pyorrhea and sore gums.	Use as a tea (one teaspoon in boiling water).	If taken for a long time, can cause low blood sugar
Pau d'Arco (Taheebo Tea)	Anti-microbial, anti-viral, anti-bacterial; boosts immune defense. Effective against Candidiasis.	Source: the inner bark of a tree in Brazil and Ecuador; used for ages by the native Indians for health problems.	Use as rinse, douche, or topically. Dilute solution. Use Taheebo as a tea.	Can cause liver distress if too much is taken, or taken too long, because it produces too much heat..

Where dosages on products in Categories II-IV are not listed, refer to product label.

II. DETOXIFICATION TO RID THE BODY OF METABOLIC WASTES

Cell Guard
(Superoxide Dismutase=S.O.D.)

The only company presently selling this form of food complex is Biotec. Biotec sells an antioxidant enzyme complex product made from special Indian wheat, claimed to be 700 times more potent than the average S.O.D. found in stores. If taken while using H_2O_2, but far enough apart so they don't cancel each other, it has been theorized that the two work together as a "dynamic duo," cleaning out the body, preventing free radical damage (such as premature aging), boosting the immune system, removing disease.

The aim is to get the oxygen into the system in a form the body can utilize, and at the same time protect the basic healthy tissue of the system from the oxidative process by using enzymes. There have been anecdotal reports attesting that this is how the combination works, and more research is needed to explore these fantastic combinations.

"Evidence of the effectiveness of enzymes taken orally is beginning to overwhelm skeptics. Much of the evidence comes from many years of studies performed in West Germany, Switzerland, Austria, Italy and Mexico. Many of these studies show that enzymes, when taken orally, demonstrate benefits against circulating immune complexes, rheumatic disorders, and auto-immune diseases."— *Peter R. Rothschild, M.D.*

Fitness Fuel

Fitness Fuel is also by Biotec. It is composed of anti-oxidant enzymes which specialize in removing heavy metals from the liver and energizing the body. These enzymes are: catalase, reducatase, and methatase.

The liver produces well over 1600 secretions. Consequently, in its ability to filter the blood, it can pick up or scavenge heavy metals, which can severely damage the body's ability to effectively dispel metabolic wastes, and also clear out free radicals.

Liva-Tox

With most opportunistic infections, there is liver damage first.

If hepatitis was present prior to the opportunistic infection, this category of supplements should be used.

Liva-Tox (by Enzymatic Therapy) has vitamins, minerals, herbs, detoxifying agents and natural virucides, which all help to remove infection and strengthen liver function.

LIV. 52 Herbal Formula

This is an ancient formula, imported from India. The ingredients are: Capers, Chicory, Wonderberry, Myrobalan, Senna, Yarrow, Manna, and Organically Complexed Iron. 100% Herbal, from the Himalaya Mountains, it has been successfully used against the deterioration of liver cells in conditions of: (1) Cirrhosis; (2) Radiation poisoning; (3) Hepatitis.

This is a liver detoxifier and rebuilder. The liver is the largest internal organ in the body, and when the liver is damaged, serious problems result, including immuno-suppression. To keep the liver healthy is a primary goal.

In my research with innumerable patients, immuno-suppression almost always involves liver damage, affected either by disease, toxins or functional damage, due to infection.

Ayurvedic (from "life" and "science") Medicine is the traditional Indian medicine. It strives to maintain an internal homeostatis. LIV.52 provides nutritional support and detoxification for the liver.

Dosage: 2-3 tablets 3 times a day.

Glutathione

Glutathione is a water-soluble amino acid used as an anti-oxidant which detoxifies (harmful) peroxides. Free radical fighter.

Immuno-suppressed persons have a Glutathione deficiency of at least 50%, according to a 1989 study, documented in *Lancet*, journal of the British Medical Assn.

Silymarin Plus

Silymarin (by Enzymatic Therapy) contains milk thistle, artichoke leaf powder, and cumin root. This product detoxifies the liver; it is also used for toxic mushroom poisoning.

Thioctic Acid (Lipoic Acid)

This product contains non-toxic nutrient B-Vitamin co-factors which oxidize serious poisons collected in the liver. Experiments have shown a quantum yield of oxygen production after using this product. Specifically, thioctic acid removes mercury, arsenobenzoles, carbon tetrachloride, and aniline dyes. It normalizes liver enzymes.

DMG Plus

DMG Plus is Di-Methylglycine (Vitamin B-15) plus TMG (Tri-Methylglycine.)

It oxygenates the blood, rids the body of uric acid, and detoxifies the body of wastes. It increases hemoglobin (red blood cell) count, and keeps anaerobic and aerobic bacteria in check, benefitting the immune system.

Phytobiotic Herbal Formula

by Enzymatic Therapy

This formula rids the body of many parasites; it is especially good for parasitic infections—E. coli, giardia, cryptosporidium .

This product is to be used in conjunction with colonics/colemics.

Lymphatic 25

Lymphatic 25 eliminates most lymphatic swellings in about 10 days. See bottle for dosage. (For swellings in neck, armpits, and groin areas.)

Intestinalis

Intestinalis is a special formula containing 22 herbs which are known to control or kill giardia, entoamoeba, and other intestinal parasites. This preparation was formulated by Dr. Louis Parrish, M. D., a foremost authority on intestinal parasites, as well as the creator of a very accurate and convenient method of testing for these parasites— the "Rectal Swab Technique."

The synergistic action of these herbs is also effective against many strains of pathogenic bacteria responsible for "Traveler's Diarrhea," and is recommended as a preventative measure on trips to any location where these bacteria flourish.

(See page 85 for source.)

Pancreatin (Mega-Zyme)

Contains digestive enzymes, taken with meals, helps reduce and eliminate food allergies. However, taking pancreatin enzymes between meals purifies the blood, eliminates food sources for the viruses, and actually digests them. The best product on the market is Mega-Zyme #425 (Enzymatic Therapy.) It contains lysozyne and chymotripsin. This last enzyme digests cancer cells.

Dosage: 4-6 tablets between meals.

Laurisine

Laurisine is a product that contains Monolaurin and Lysine. It is non-toxic, and works directly on the envelope coat of the virus. It interferes with viral attachment to host cells.

Viricidin contains Monolaurin in a base of BHT and Zinc Picolinate. BHT has successfully activated the lipid envelope virus. Low concentrations of BHT have therapeutic effectiveness against all Herpes viruses.

Suggestion: Use only one of these three: Monolaurin, Laurisine, or Viricidin.

Sea Klenz Intestinal Cleansers

The digestive tract is as much a lifeline of the body as the bloodstream. Today, the average diet is filled with chemicals and preservatives, over-processed foods and a lack of fiber.

Wachters' Sea Klenz Intestinal Cleansers are specifically formulated to counteract some of these harmful effects, and will help promote proper digestion and elimination, remove stagnation and maintain daily colon health. They are all natural, non-habit forming, bulk fiber cleansers, whose main ingredient is organic sea vegetation.

Sea Klenz is non-abrasive, soothing, and is used for: (1) constipation, or to prevent same; (2) malabsorption; and (3) a preparation for the colonic regime.

The ingredients of the original formula (called 51-B) are: A combination of Sodium Alginate from sea vegetation; Psyllium seed husks; dehydrated lemon powder; cereal solids, and a Wachters' blend of sea plants. Sea Klenz is not found in stores.

(See page 85 for source.)

Taheebo Tea
(from Lapachol/Pau d'Arco)

One woman with Candidiasis was using the doctor-prescribed drug nystatin. After drinking Taheebo Tea for four months, her need for the drug was eliminated. In other cases, skin rashes and athlete's foot disappeared.

Lapachol is from a most unusual South American tree. It lives in tropical forests where bacteria and fungi thrive, yet the tree is free from most parasites. The native Indians since Inca days have used the inner bark of the tree to combat internal and external infections. The tree is called Ipe roxo and Pau d'Arco in Brazil, Taheebo in Bolivia and Lapacho in Argentina.

Dr. Theodore Meyer discovered the tree in Argentina and now grows these trees in his wilderness plantations in that country, 100% organically, ecologically, without any chemicals.

The active ingredient in the inner bark of this tree is called Lapachol. It is effective in combating gram-positive, an acid-fast bacteria and fungus. Topically, it can be applied to sores and lesions with benefit.

Quinones, alkaloids developed from plants, have many anti-cancer properties, and Lapachol has a full range of quinones.

Tree-Tea Oil
(Oil of Melaleuca alternifolia)

This powerful, eucalyptus-like oil is an antiseptic, and eliminates bacteria and fungi without injuring healthy tissue. In studies performed in Australia, the U.S. and France, tree-tea oil was found useful to eliminate a broad spectrum of pesky infestations, yeast infection, athlete's foot, lice, ringworm, trichomoniasis, acne, etc.

It contains several natural chemical constituents found nowhere else in the herbal kingdom. In Australia, its source, it is called "a first-aid kit in a bottle." Tree-tea oil has many uses, and is found in most U.S. health food stores.

Wild Yam Root
(Dioscorea villosa)

This Chinese herb is used by women in Mexico for natural birth control. It has antiviral properties and balances female hormones. Now available in the U. S. in capsule form, it is safe to use, with no harmful side effects.

Source: Living Earth, 731 E. Howard St., Boone, NC 28607. Phone (704) 264-1504. It is modest in cost. A booklet, *Birth Control Without Fear* by Willa Schaeffer, is also available from this source.

Lymphatic Arm Swings

Like skiing down a slope, swing the arm, from above the head to behind the back, 200 times a day.

Upside Down Bicycle Pumping

Back is flat on the floor, with knees bent. This is for lymphatic swelling in the groin area. Since lymphatic vessels flow in the opposite direction of the blood vessels, exercises have to be inverted, as mentioned above. These exercises drain the lymphatic fluids from the areas of congestion.

Walking as Exercise

The value of exercise is well known. We would like to remind our readers of the joys of walking, a most simple exercise, without cost, that can be done anywhere at any time.

A book that tells all about it is *Complete Book of Exercise Walking*, by Gary D. Yanker. The author writes: "Walking is a dynamic action that uses almost all of the body's 206 bones and 650 muscles. . . . . Studies have shown how a walking program can contribute to physical fitness and overall health." The book is a basic manual for learning how to convert your existing walking activities into exercise. Yanker writes: "Walking changed my life. I learned that walking makes you relax and get in touch with yourself and the outside world." A most interesting and useful story he tells is that of a fellow walker and friend who was a heavy smoker. No amount of persuasion could cause him to even think of stopping. But some heavy walking so oxygenated his body that the craving for nicotine just fell away by itself.

There are nationwide walking clubs.

Pre-Colonic Information

The small intestine is the area where most food absorption occurs. Its parts are: the duodenum and the anterior portion, including the jejunum and the ileum.

The main function of the large intestine is the absorption of water. It consists of these parts: the cecum, the ascending colon, the transverse colon, the descending colon, the sigmoid colon, the rectum, and the anal canal—forming a kind of frame around the abdominal cavity.

In preparing for a colonic, no food should be consumed for at least ten hours. Upon awakening, or at least three hours before the colonic, Wachters' Sea Klenz should be taken.

The purpose in taking an intestinal cleanser prior to a colonic is that the colonic empties the large intestine of wastes, bacteria, etc., but not the small intestine. Sea Klenz helps to push (like a broom) fecal material and wastes from the small intestine, where the colonic does not act.

Herbal Fiber #750 and #751 by Enzymatic Therapy also contain ingredients that help rid the body of parasites and yeast overgrowth.

The colemic cleansing process is a gradual one, and after the bowels are cleaned, the water loosens caked-up residues on the inside lining. The bacteria mucus-ridden excrement is expelled into the toilet, where it belongs! Patience is necessary, because the body is not always ready to release its poisons all at once.

You must be willing to do this — in order to heal your body!

There are many positive effects from colon cleansing. One is that the lymphatics become unblocked, appetite is regained, absorption is greatly increased, mental abilities are improved, the eyes clear, one can work longer hours without fatigue, the disposition improves. (Toxins make one irritable, angry, sluggish, mean!)

And, of course, toxins make one sick. It is truly said that "death begins in the colon."

The people of the world are polluted within — and this causes antagonisms and strife — because the internal toxins make people angry, as well as sick.

This is so important that we wish to emphasize it: **Colonics and Colemics not only cleanse the body but the mind!** When the body is loaded with toxins (and everyone's is — unless they are cleaning the colon constantly) — the person becomes irritable and angry — the toxins affect the mind.

Contrariwise, after a colon cleansing, one becomes kind, amiable, loving — as well as getting a big surge of energy.

We must not only eat properly but assimilate and eliminate.

Mere emptying the bowels on the toilet is not enough. You have a choice of a *Colemic* (at home — you do the process yourself, or with the help of a family member)— or a *Colonic* (where you go to the office of a health practitioner who gives colonics).

Just one of either will not do the job! The first few times you have the colonic or colemic (the latter is more thorough) — you will notice that the process helps soften and carry away intestinal debris. But the real cleansing comes after this intestinal putrefaction is removed, and one actually gets down to the mucus in the lining of the intestines.

Research has demonstrated that the colon has reflex points that affect the organs — so the physical process of the water entering and being expelled has a toning effect — not only on the intestinal system, but also on stimulating the various organs.

A well-developed tissue cleansing system is very good to help overcome pain in all parts of the body.

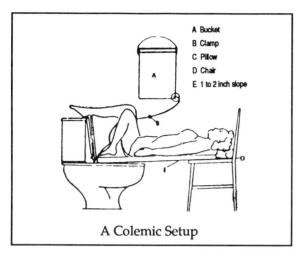

A Colemic Setup

In working to overcome a serious degenerative disease, it is recommended that the treatment be ongoing and constantly applied. Every other day is best, for the first week. If the patient drops in energy suddenly, the process must be halted.

It should be understood that this treatment is not a cure-all, but an important step in the detoxification program.

This detoxification program is very powerful. Tremendous healing can be accomplished!

Not all the toxins are expelled. Some of them go back into the system. Therefore, if it is at all possible, go into a wet sauna — the same or the next day. Those toxins which are in the circulatory system are pushed out through the skin.

Benefits of Colonics and Colemics

After a colonic or colemic, (or series of them), you can expect:
(1) Your eyes to lighten in color;
(2) Sores on the body to heal more quickly;
(3) Increased energy;
(4) Clearer thinking;
(5) A general feeling of well-being;
(6) The skin will glow with radiance;
(7) Joint and back pain will lessen;
(8) Darker skin on the genitals and rectum will lighten (the dark flesh indicates blood stagnation);
(9) The appetite will increase;

(10) An extended stomach will be reduced, with repeated treatments;
(11) Much Candida Albicans and bacteria will be washed out of the colon;
(12) You will achieve a more youthful appearance.

It is advisable to use Chromium Complex (hypoallergenic) after a colonic/colemic. The ingredients of this product are: Glutathione and Niacin. Chromium helps regulate blood sugar levels. Also use Bacillus Laterosporous (2 tablespoons in 2 oz. of water).

A colonic or colemic can temporarily make you feel weak because a tremendous amount of toxins are eliminated from the body. When the body is healing, energy is consumed.

It is advisable to take your colemic before retiring, so that the body can rest and heal.

Instructions for the Colemic

Upon receiving your colemic board, assemble according to instructions. Purchase a five-gallon plastic bucket with a handle.

The colemic board can be positioned at any angle, so it fits in virtually any bathroom. The part of the board with the catheter rests on the toilet seat, and the back of the board rests on a chair or the bathtub.

Wash the bucket with hydrogen peroxide or bleach. Get it super clean. The bucket must be at least three feet above the board. It can be placed on a table, wooden box or crate or improvised in some way. It could be suspended from a hook in the ceiling. Half fill the bucket before suspending it. Use water as warm as possible, but watch the temperature. If the water is hot to your hand, it will be hotter to the rectum. Warm water expands the intestine, and allows for much more rapid expulsion of toxic wastes.

Filling the hose: First, clamp the hose. One end of the hose has a plastic "L"; turn the hose upside down. This part has a metal weight in it. You are going to start pouring water into the rubber tube. As soon as one section is filled, unclamp and pour more water in; then reclamp. In other words, the entire tube has to be totally filled with water. The air must be out of the tube. It works by reverse gravity. It is called siphoning.

The next step: fill the bucket to top, using another container to do so. Then put thumb over top of rubber tube (you don't want any air to get in or water to get out), and invert it, place the weighted tube into the bucket. It will go right down to the bottom.

Insert the catheter into the rectum approximately two inches.

You are ready for your colemic!

The water will enter and exit with fecal matter from the rectum. The advantages over an enema are:

(1) You control the water temperature. You can add more hot or cold water to your bucket;

(2) You don't have to get up until the five gallons of water are used;

(3) You may add herbs, chlorophyll, etc.;

(4) You can do implants with the colemic board;

(5) You can change your position: you can sit up, you can lie down, you can turn to your right side or left side; you can have your knees up and bent, or legs straight.

(6) As the water enters, you can release it at any time by pushing out. You can allow the water to go further by taking a deep breath and expanding your abdomen; permit the water to go up as far as you desire. If there is too much pressure, there is fecal blockage.

(7) The intestine has pockets called villi (finger-like projections), where these toxins and poisons are trapped, so don't expect it to happen all at once. You will have a major breakthrough! You can't expect to do just one intestinal cleaning.

(8) You can massage different parts of your body; this triggers the release of the fecal matter. Your thumb or finger can be placed on a hard mass, which will start pulsating and trigger a release. Then you might exclaim:"Oh, what a feeling!"

(9) Letting go of fecal matter, toxins, and poisons physically can also simultaneously release *mental* poisons and toxins. This release is a total catharsis.

(10) While this is going on, you can declare, mentally or audibly: "I am letting go of old things in my life I no longer need; they no longer belong there. I feel strong. I have no fear. I am clean!"

Implants

Implants should not be attempted with a dirty colon, because you will reabsorb the toxins. After some intestinal cleaning, perhaps three weeks, implantation can be attempted.

Another name for implants is rectal feeding. Nutrients are absorbed very readily through the rectum. Rectal feeding differs from a colonic in that nutritional liquids are implanted into the rectum, and held for 5-15 minutes. Substances that can be used: herbs, garlic (macerate and add to water); chlorophyll; herbal teas. One rule: never irritate the mucous membrane. The substances should be soothing, healing, not irritating. Don't make the solutions too strong. H_2O_2 should only be attempted under the supervision of a health professional.

Bacillus Laterosporous liquid may be used as an implant after several colemics.

The Sauna

The sauna increases detoxification by inducing artificial fever. It speeds up circulation and body cell metabolism, thus causing toxic wastes to be expelled through the skin.

Steps in a Sauna

First and foremost, the sauna must be a steam sauna, not dry. It must be warm enough for profuse sweating but not uncomfortable (should be relaxing, not painfully hot.)

Because individuals have different heat tolerances, we cannot specify here what temperature the steam should be, nor how long to stay.

In Finland, dry heat is not used — only wet saunas.

The Process:

One wraps himself in a towel and sits or reclines. Shortly, perspiration will commence.

At this time, massage painful areas of your body. The pores will be open. Now, to facilitate the eliminating process, the dead skin can be rubbed away with the fingers or a brush. The more dead skin is removed, the more the pores will be opened.

Now you leave the steam room. Let the body cool down gradually (no cold plunge or shower). Lie down and rest, at least half an hour. Now you get up and rinse in lukewarm water, scrubbing the skin again. Finally, you can use very cold water and use a rough towel to dry yourself. Allow enough time for the pores to close.

Go at least twice a week.

Cautions

• Immuno-suppressed individuals especially should be sure that the sauna is clean. If the sauna appears to be unclean, ask the attendant to hose it down for you.

• As the body detoxifies via the lungs and skin, toxic odors can be produced through perspiration and respiration.

• The best conditions are to be in the sauna alone or with only one other person, not many. Avoid people who are coughing, expectorating phlegm, expelling gas, and releasing discharge of all kinds.

• Also, if you can find it, go to a sauna with purified or mineral water, rather than to those which use tap water with chlorine, etc.

• Never chill yourself; dry yourself thoroughly and allow the body to cool down slowly.

• Wear thongs or rubber shoes to protect yourself from athlete's foot, etc.

• Don't stay too long; if you feel weak or tired, you should leave the sauna.

• Before entering the sauna, you may take 500-1000 mgs of niacin, which is a vaso-dilator of the skin capillaries. Niacin opens the blood vessels, allowing body toxins to be pushed through the skin.

• Drink plenty of distilled water while in the sauna, to help wash the toxins out.

Liver and Gall Bladder Flush

The liver is one of the most important organs, with multiple functions. The largest glandular structure in the body, it manufactures hormones and blood protein. It creates the clotting mechanism for the blood and filters the blood. It manufactures, stores and secretes vitamins and other nutrients.

This flush improves the immune system by detoxifying the liver and gall bladder. It is a powerful rejuvenator and acts as an important detoxifying agent which helps to restore the normal function of these two organs by flushing out stones from the gall bladder and hepatic duct.

Many persons with stones do not realize they have them. (This flush is not recommended for conditions of diagnosed large stones.) The author himself used this flush successfully; many stones left his body after he gave himself his first flush. This spared him the necessity of having surgery.

Steps in Flush Treatment:

Monday through Saturday noon: Drink as much apple juice or apple cider as your appetite will permit in addition to regular meals and any supplements you are taking. Try to locate apple juice or cider without additives; purchase the natural type in a health food store.

Saturday noon: eat a normal lunch.

Three hours later, take one tablespoon of magnesium sulphate (Epsom Salt) dissolved in 1/4 cup warm water. Or use Laci Le Beau Tea (also called Super Dieter's Tea). These laxatives create a peristalsis of the lower bowel, causing any stones to be passed. If the taste of the above products is objectionable to you, drink a little orange juice or grapefruit juice, freshly squeezed if possible.

Two hours later, repeat the step in the paragraph above.

For Saturday's dinner, use a citrus juice for the meal.

At bedtime, drink 1/2 cup of warm unrefined olive oil (extra-virgin is best) blended with 1/2 cup of lemon juice (fresh and organic, if possible).

After this you should go to bed immediately. Lie on your right side with your knees pulled up close to your chest for 30 minutes.

The next morning, one hour before breakfast, take one tablespoon of magnesium sulphate (Epsom Salt) dissolved in 1/4 cup warm water.

Continue with your normal diet and any nutritional program prescribed for you.

Occasionally, persons who take this flush report slight to moderate nausea from the olive oil/lemon juice combination. This nausea will slowly disappear by the time you go to sleep. If the olive oil induces vomiting, you need not repeat the procedure at this time. This occurs only in rare instances. The flushing of the liver and gall bladder stimulates and cleanses these organs as no other method can do.

Persons who have chronically suffered from gallstones, biliousness, backaches, nausea, etc., occasionally find small gallstone-type objects in the stool the following day. These stones are from light green to dark green in color. They are irregular in shape and vary in size from that of grape seeds to cherry seeds. If there seems to be a large number of these stones in the stool, the liver flush should be repeated in two weeks. Gallstones form when there is too much fat in the diet.

Remember, if you are employed, you need not take time off work. Simply devote a Saturday or Sunday to this flush. No fasting is required. This flush is a highly important self-treatment. When the liver works well, the whole body usually functions well. There is also a claim by some holistic doctors that cleansing the liver helps to cancel addictions.

Parasites and People

Immuno-suppression weakens the body's ability to fight off different parasites. Often, immuno-suppressed individuals have different microbes interacting with each other, possibly even living off each other. It is vitally important to rid the body of these parasites.

Giardia lamblia and *Entoamoeba histolitica* are the most common parasites that reside in our bodies, depriving us of nourishment and energy.

The signs of parasite infection are: (1) loss of weight; (2) abnormal, voracious appetite; (3) the urge to eat very often; (4) rectal itching; (5) diarrhea. It is not surprising that many HIV-Positive individuals and Candidiasis and Herpes patients have parasites.

Parasites are very difficult to detect in the body, and Occult Stool Specimens for Ova is not the best detector of infestation. An anal rectal smear—actually taking the rectal mucosa—is much more accurate. Nevertheless, this test is not an easy one to perform. It takes a specialist, and even that test is not always accurate.

Parasites can be present anywhere in the body. Consequently, if they are not in the digestive tract or stool, they can go undetected. These parasites often transform themselves—change from one form to another (this is called pleomorphism). They often do not have a cell membrane that is easily stained to be viewed under microscopic examination in the laboratory. Parasites can be eliminated when conditions are no longer favorable for their existence. This can be done by disrupting their cycle, changing their food, changing the environmental pH, electrocuting them, or poisoning them with substances that do not harm the rest of the body.

Parasites in America are a larger problem than most people realize. Not even doctors can recognize most parasitic conditions, as they are not trained in diagnosing and treating them. Doctors often diagnose such cases as bacterial infections and treat them with antibiotics, but these drugs have no effect on most parasites.

Even with the general wealth, high standard of living and cleanliness in the U.S., parasites are a huge problem—sometimes even reaching epidemic proportions. The Centers for Disease Control state that virtually every known parasitic disease has been found in the U.S.

SOURCES OF PARASITIC INFECTIONS:

Parasites can invade the body from eating undercooked pork (these are tapeworms); from eating rare steaks; from pets; from shaking hands with an infected person; from raw vegetables on which eggs are laid*; from sexual activities; from eating in restaurants where food handlers are careless in sanitation. (*Scrape or peel raw vegetables before eating them.)

MAJOR FACTORS:

Lack of sanitation; colons that are clogged and impacted from years of improper eating habits and lack of cleansing the colon. Such a location is ideal as a breeding ground for parasites and worms. They proliferate in environments like this: dark, warm, and with a constant supply of nourishment—the rich remains of mankind's food. The creatures can feed unlimitedly, and thus they multiply without restraint. Usually the colon owner is entirely oblivious of what is going on in his system. The wastes are absorbed into the bloodstream of the human host and carried to all parts of the body causing illness which is often misdiagnosed.

TYPES OF PARASITES PREVALENT IN THE U.S.:

Giardia lamblia, a protozoan parasite, most prevalent. It is considered the main cause of waterborne disease. Symptoms are: diarrhea, weakness, weight loss, abdominal cramps, belching, fever, nausea. The single-celled parasites can coat the inside lining of the small intestine and prevent it from absorbing nutrients from food.

THE TAPEWORM:

If tapeworms multiply to become very numerous, they cause intestinal obstruction and intestinal distress. Tapeworm eggs in the liver can be mistaken for cancer.

BLOODFLUKES:

These are often found in AIDS patients. They make lesions in the lungs and cause hemorrhages under the skin. They can cause arthritis-like pains or leukemia-like symptoms, and generally weaken the entire system.

TREATMENT:

Colon cleaning is the principal way to eliminate parasites in the large intestine. At the same time, the impacted wastes are cleaned out. A series of colonics or colemics is required. Filtered water should be used. The beneficial effects are many. Read the entire section on colonics and colemics in this book carefully.

If you suspect that you have parasites in the colon, start a cleansing program soon. It is inexpensive (no cost for colemics after you buy your own equipment), it is simple, and is one of the most marvelous things you could possibly do for your health.

DIAGNOSIS:

The proper, accurate diagnosis of the various parasites is now known to be technically difficult and demands skill and experience. It may take more than one attempt to accurately confirm or deny the presence of parasites.

An accurate method of testing may involve a combination of stool samples and a rectal mucus sample, taken with a swab over a period of several days.

There are several excellent test labs with experience in culturing stool samples for hard-to-find parasites. Two of them are the Great Smokies Laboratory, and Meridian Valley Laboratory.

All testing must be done under the supervision of a skilled health practitioner with experience in taking samples to be sent to these labs, which do not accept samples directly from patients.

Invisible Parasites and Other Dangers from Swimming

Most people do not realize the dangers of swimming in fresh waters in certain localities. A disease called Schistosomiasis (also known as bilharzia) comes from parasites living in snails that inhabit the fresh waters of Africa, Brazil, China, the Caribbean, Puerto Rico, Southeast Asia, the Middle East, and Suriname.

Robert Wittes, M.D., of the division of parasitic diseases at the Centers for Disease Control in Atlanta, says that schisto (the abbreviated name) is the most serious problem fresh water swimmers encounter. He adds that the disease is difficult—sometimes even impossible—to diagnose.

"Someone might develop general aches and pains, which could progress to a cough and a fever, or to an infection of the urinary or gastro–intestinal tract. Or a person could simply be asymptomatic, then go on to develop fatal liver or kidney disease," states Dr. Wittes.

Some schisto parasites are extremely resistant; they can remain in a human system for up to 20 years. There is no preventive or totally curative drug at the present time.

Wittes recommends asking advice from a reputable person—a tour director, public health official or doctor—in the area. But do not take guidance from the local population. "In Africa you will see natives swimming in streams or lakes that are infested. Some have partial immunity, but most of them have the disease," adds Wittes.

Other health problems that can develop from swimming in fresh waters, even in the U.S., are viral hepatitis A, viral gastroenteritis and eye or ear infections, says Wittes. Water can be contaminated by human and/or industrial waste in all parts of the world.

The solution is simple: if there is any doubt about the purity of the waters, don't take a chance.

(See page 24 for summary of "Intestinalis" formula for parasitic conditions.)

III. INCREASING CELLULAR METABOLISM TO ENERGIZE THE BODY

Km (Matol Corp.)

Km is a special potassium preparation that regulates the blood chemistry and biological balance. It helps remove toxicity from the bloodstream, keeping the blood vessels clean. Km has herbal and therapeutic properties that accelerate the rate of chemical reactions in the bloodstream. It is a very rich source of trace elements, minerals and organic acids that enrich the blood.

The immune system is found not only in one organ or gland, but throughout the entire body. Km nourishes the blood, which courses through the glands, and greatly influences them.

Km was developed by an agrobiologist, Karl Jurak, in Austria. The principal ingredients are: alfalfa, angelica root, cascara sagrada, celery seed, chamomile flowers, dandelion root, gentian root, horehound root, licorice root, passion flower, sarsaparilla root, saw palmetto berry, senega root, and thyme.

The following are excerpts from a talk by Karl Jurak:

"The bloodstream benefits from Km to a degree that is almost unbelievable. Km purifies the bloodstream, removes the toxins and the impurities at the rim of the blood vessels. This we call cholesterol, which causes a film that prevents the food value to enter the blood vessels, and also creates rigid veins.

"As you know, systolic and peristaltic functions are essential for the heart to pump blood into the veins. The veins must be elastic enough to squeeze and pump the blood back to the heart, then going to the lungs, becoming oxygenated.

"When we inhale, we inhale much oxygen, but we exhale the oxygen immediately, and much is lost.

"Now, this is what happens when Km is used. I have verified it over and over again. For some unknown reason, with Km use, a great deal more oxygen is retained with each intake of breath. Consequently, the blood becomes oxygenated to a far greater extent.

"This oxygen goes to your brain cells and activates the brain. It is important that the blood be so regenerated because *the blood is the stream of life and the most potent living substance in the body.* This is a new type of feeding to the cells and to the entire metabolism, and because of that, we find that every gland and every cell is affected.

"Thousands of times I have heard this: 'My feet were as cold as ice for years and years, but now they are perfectly warm. I have perfect circulation now,' and so on. The people find that the blood reaches all extremities. In place of the blue tones of the skin, inadequately fed with circulated blood, people get warm and pink skin tones. Circulation is one of the main things that is accomplished with oxygenating the blood. In 60 years, I have never seen this product fail once in helping do some good for the people using it."

—Dr. Karl Jurak, creator of Km.

Note: Some medical doctors recommend Km for Candida and other yeast conditions, and for Pre-Menstrual Syndrome.

34 •

Exsula
(Quantum Advance, Int'l)

In the human body, there are many types of enzymes. They help break down our food to smaller components for easy assimilation.

Different kinds of enzymes in our bloodstream transport micro-nutrients to the blood, and thus to the nerves, muscles and glands. Enzymes have other vital functions that deal with immunity, detoxification, removal of wastes, sexual reproduction, sugar storage and metabolism, and elimination of carbon dioxide in the lungs.

Enzyme depletion, coupled with a systemic acid-alkaline imbalance, is a foundation for immune system disorders.

The new product Exsula is loaded with enzymes which provide a food-based foundation for nutritional fortification of the immune system.

Exsula is a highly concentrated drink containing: green barley juice; green wheat grass juice; Hawaiian spirulina; Co-enzyme Q10; Royal Jelly; Dunaliella Carotene; Soya Lecithin; Antioxidant Enzymes (Superoxide Dismutase, Methione Reductase, Glutathione Peroxidase and Catalase); Soluble Apple Fiber; Vitamin B-12; Gamma Linolenic Acid; RNA/DNA, plus essential vitamins and minerals.

Exsula is a formulation of enzyme-rich plant extracts and sea vegetation. It is from food concentrates, and contains no synthetics. It supplies nutritional support to help increase energy, lower blood pressure, cleanse the body, and is totally vegetarian. It has a mild laxative effect. It is used by some to stimulate mental abilities. Exsula may be taken in a variety of liquids, or by dissolving in the mouth. It is better sipped than gulped. (For source, see page 85.)

Optimum Liquid Minerals
(Integrated Health)

An ancient sea bed is the source of these minerals. Because they are liquid, they are easily assimilated.

Minerals are catalysts (substances that stimulate a chemical reaction without altering the original substance).

Optimum Liquid Minerals are taken with or after meals because they aid in digestion. Due to their catalytic action, they aid in food absorption and assimilation.

Dosage: 2 to 4 ounces in distilled water, with or after meals.

Raw Adrenal Complex
(#403 Enzymatic Therapy)

Used for fatigue, stress and weakness, and weak adrenal glands. Ingredients: raw adrenal and adrenal cortex; raw pituitary; Betaine; L-Tyrosine; Vitamin C; Vitamin B-6; Pantothenic Acid.

Dosage: take one capsule twice a day.

In more severe conditions, the product to be used is:

Adrenal Cortex Complex
(#408-A, Enzymatic Therapy)

For adrenal weakness and general malaise. The product is stronger than the previous one. It is soluble, raw, adrenal cortex plus predigested glandular extracts.

Raw adrenal cortex contains raw liver, raw duodenum, raw pancreas, raw pituitary, raw thymus, raw brain, plus tyrosine.

Dosage: start with one or two capsules daily.

Other products to support the adrenals are Vitamin C— 5,000 to 10,000 mgs. daily and Pantothenic Acid — 500 to 1,000 mgs. daily.

Ester-C with Mineral Formula

Ester-C is a unique, patented Vitamin C formulation known as a "Polyascorbate," which is more effectively utilized by the body than other comparable Vitamin C supplements.

Ester-C is made from vital minerals, most commonly Calcium, fully reacted in a ratio of 10 parts Ascorbic acid to 1 part mineral. The mineral buffers the formula, and the pH is 6.9-7.1, which is similar to that of distilled water. This product is well tolerated by those with sensitive intestinal tracts.

In addition, Ester-C contains naturally occurring "metabolites" of Vitamin C, which are unique to the product, and which tests show increase the amount of C absorbed and the length of retention in the blood, and allow dosage to be decreased by half or more of that of other C formulas.

Dosage of Vitamin C varies widely, with high daily doses in the 8-20 gram range often used for more severe opportunistic infections, and maintenance doses in the 1-5 gram daily range.

It is important to divide the daily total into as many doses per day as possible, between a minimum of 3 to a maximum of 12.

Liquid Liver
(Enzymatic Therapy)

Rebuilds liver cells, thus stimulating energy. Take 6-8 capsules per day. It can be taken with foods.

Procaine (GH-3)

This is a non-toxic substance discovered by a woman doctor in Rumania, Dr. Ana Aslan. It stimulates the adrenal glands, is a lipidtropic enhancer. It is chemically broken down into PABA and DMAE. Basically, it gives the body energy. It may retard the body aging process by its MAO inhibition, which detoxifies the brain and nervous system.

Ultravital H-4

Ultravital H-4 is being used successfully in the U. S. S. R. and is a formulation of the Soviet Institute of Medical Sciences. It is specifically for athletic performance, for increased energy and stamina.

Athletes have found that H-4 assists in physical strength and performance. It is similar in composition to Procaine (GH-3). It stimulates tissue regeneration and improves the metabolic processes. The product has also been proven as an oxidation reduction phenomenon of the cells.

Ultravital H-4 contains the same ingredients as GH-3 plus Calcium Pangamate, Vitamin B-12, Trimethylglycine. TMG oxygenates the cells and is much stronger than GH-3.

Selenium

Selenium deficiencies have been linked to limited immune response against Candidiasis. Phagocytes (cells that eat bacteria) require selenium as an essential co-factor for their Glutathione peroxidase enzyme. It has been demonstrated experimentally that selenium deficiency selectively predisposes people to yeast infection.

Dosage: See label on container.

Note: Selenium is toxic in doses greater than suggested by manufacturers.

Magnesium

Low levels of vaginal magnesium have been associated with increased staphylococcus toxins and with toxic shock syndrome and Candidiasis.

Reverse ratio has proven to be more effective.

Most supplements have a 2:1 ratio (two parts calcium to one part magnesium in this case) but with magnesium a reverse ratio has proven to be more effective — 1:2 (one part calcium to 2 parts magnesium).

Dosages: follow directions on container.

Atomodine

A water-soluble iodine compound containing Iodine Trichloride. Valuable because the iodine is in a form less toxic to the body than molecular iodine. It must be taken internally with care. It can be harmful to anyone who takes too large a dose.

Each drop of Atomodine supplies approximately six times the minimum daily requirement of iodine. Too much iodine can lead to overstimulation of the thyroid gland, resulting in nervousness, insomnia, and rapid heartbeat. Even a skin rash can result from too much iodine taken over a period of time.

Dosage: one drop in a glass of water. Take for 3 days, then stop for a period of time.

Natural Energy Tonic
(Home Preparation)

Add one tablespoon of blackstrap molasses and one tablespoon of fresh lemon juice to a cup of warm water. Take up to three times a day.

Multi-GP

Multi-GP is a hypo-allergenic, sub-lingual "B" vitamin and mineral supplement complex that is totally absorbed and bio-active. It is an extremely important supplement to be taken when the body is weak or run down.

Dosage: 1/2 teaspoon to 1 teaspoon as a dietary supplement 1/2 hour before or 2 hours after a meal. The bottle contains 7 oz. or 200 grams. It dissolves quickly; it may be held 30-60 seconds under the tongue. No toxicity.

Amino-HE

Amino-HE is a unique nutritional supplement of crystalline pre-formed amino acids. It is extremely high in L-Glutamic Acid, which stimulates proper brain function, and as amino acids are the building blocks of proteins, often when an individual is in a weakened or sickened state, he is not absorbing his nutrients properly, especially amino acids. Very pure; no corn, wheat, soy, binders or fillers. Take it sub-lingually (under the tongue); it dissolves quickly. It can be taken with Multi-GP. Both taste good.

Dosage: For adults, about 1 1/2 teaspoons 1/2 hour before or 2 hours after meals. Place under the tongue. Children from 4 to 12 can take it. The bottle contains 200 grams of 21 individual packets.

Vitol-27

This all-herbal tonic, made in Canada by Vital International, was created from 27 optimum herbs, selected from around the world. Herbs work best together, and the cornerstone of this unique combination is the famous Ginseng.

This tonic is unpasteurized; it gives energy, removes toxins from the blood, has laxative properties, and enhances digestion. A liquid, it is easy to take.

No claims are made for Vitol-27 beyond the fact that centuries of human experience have shown that the many herbs contained in this herbal drink act in total harmony with the human system.

Through modern research, it has been learned that herbs provide us with an amazingly rich array of organic molecules—proteins, vitamins, minerals, enzymes, lipids, sugars, alkaloids, and many other health-promoting molecules as well.

In addition to Ginseng, Vitol-27 contains Alfalfa, Avens Root, Blessed Thistle, Blue Violet Leaves, Chaparral, Culvers Root, Dandelion Root, Ginger Root, Horsetail, Hydrangea, Hyssop, Licorice Root, Marjoram, Melilot, Mullein Leaves, Myrrh, Parsley, Red Clover, Rose Hips, Rosemary, Sage, Thyme, Valerian, Watercress, Woodruff, and Yellow Dock. An optimum blend of these 27 herbs has become Vitol-27. It also contains honey and mineral-rich molasses.

For a source, please see page 85.

IV. CELLULAR REPAIR TO REBUILD THE IMMUNE SYSTEM

In any immuno-suppressed condition, infection must be addressed first. It is counter-productive to stimulate the formation or an increase of T-cells, white blood cells and interferon, unless rampant opportunistic infection is corrected first.

Example: exposure to sunlight helps the body to produce its own interferon. But when there is infection in the T-cells of a patient, he will produce *more* infection with the interferon-producing sunlight. Obviously, to spread more infection is undesirable.

The primary goal in this final step is to provide more energy to the body so that it can heal itself. Therefore, it is necessary that the sequential order in this protocol be followed.

Gold Stake

Many disorders of the body are caused by mineral shortages and imbalances. With the depletion of our soils, chemical pesticides, etc., many people are not getting proper amounts of mineral substances. Minerals act like catalysts to "turn on" different bodily mechanisms. They oxygenate the blood.

Gold Stake is a potent, water-soluble, non-toxic mineral from ancient sea beds. Research has suggested that this product increases red blood cell and bone marrow production, and is recommended for all immune disorders. Research has been done in the Netherlands; documentation reports cases of remissions of different immune disorders.

Dosage: Two capsules in the morning on an empty stomach, and two capsules in the evening on an empty stomach.

A salve is also available, helpful for skin conditions, even severe ones.

Organic Germanium

Germanium is an element found at No. 32 on the periodic table. It is naturally occurring in garlic and in Siberian ginseng.

Research shows that germanium oxygenates the cells, activates the immune system, and enhances the production of natural interferon. That germanium markedly stimulates gamma-interferon production is well documented, both in experimental and animal research. It is classified as an immuno-stimulating oxide which binds up or chelates (grabs), and removes toxic compounds harmful to the body. This chelating effect renders germanium helpful in mercury, cadmium, and similar metal poisonings.

Germanium is currently being used in other countries and research has demonstrated its efficacy for cancer, arthritis, and aging. It corrects hypoxia (lack of oxygen).

Most of the germanium sold in health food stores has too low a potency to be useful in opportunistic infections. In addition, one must always purchase only "Germanium Sesquioxide," also known as "Ge-132," and no other kind. This form has over 20 years of research and testing behind it. Pure, high quality Ge-132 does not contain contaminants such as Germanium Dioxide, which have been implicated in renal toxicity.

In research being done in Japan and West Germany, dosages of Ge-132 range from a minimum of 200 milligrams per day up, taken at least twice a day.

Germanium should not be taken continually every day for many months, as the body may build up a natural tolerance and the benefits may be lost.

Recommended: Take sublingual Ge-132, preferably tablets with as little other ingredients in them as possible. Sublingual administration increases the amount that enters the blood by a factor of about 50% over oral (swallowing).

Take one 200 mg. tablet the first day (break in half and take twice during the day). Second day, 400 mg. Third day, 600 mg. Fourth day, 800 mg. Stop for two days, then repeat the schedule starting with 200 mgs. up to 800 mgs. a day.

Black Currant Seed Oil

Black Currant Seed Oil provides essential fatty acid oils and is high in prostaglandin. It is the highest source of gammalinoleic acid. It stimulates the immune response and has anti-viral and anti-inflammatory properties.

Aloe-Vera

For over 5,000 years, Aloe Vera juice, from the Aloe Vera plant, has been regarded in folk medicine to have unique healing properties. However, Aloe has not been accepted by modern medicine. The Aloe plant is a succulent. It consists of thick green leaves with a gelatinous substance inside. Aloe juice, properly processed, contains many healing ingredients. Its principal qualities are: antiseptic, anti-inflammatory, and anti-viral, the latter a very promising feature recently discovered*.

ANTISEPTIC: The plant produces six antiseptic agents: Lupeol, a natural salicylic acid, urea nitrogen, cinnamonic acid, phenol, and sulfur. All six demonstrate antimicrobiological effects. Lupeol and salicylic acid also have analgesic effects.

ANTI-INFLAMMATORY: Aloe contains three plant sterols, which are important fatty acids—HDL cholesterol (which lowers fats in the blood), campesterol, and B-sitosterol. All are helpful in reducing symptoms of allergies and acid indigestion. These compounds also aid in arthritis, rheumatic fever, both internal and external ulcers, and inflammation of the digestive system. The stomach, small intestine, liver, kidneys and pancreas are benefitted.

ANTI-VIRAL: Most significant of all. This book brings you news of the anti-viral effects of the compound called acemannan, isolated from Aloe. *Medical World News*, December 1987 issue, contained an article entitled "Aloe Drug May Mimic AZT Without Toxicity." Dr. H. Reg McDaniel stated: "A substance in the Aloe plant shows preliminary signs of boosting AIDS patients' immune systems and blocking the human immuno-deficiency virus' spread without toxic side effects."

The drug derived from the plant is called Polymannoactate; it is currently under study. An article by Irwin Frank in the July 12, 1988 *Dallas Times Herald* quotes Dr. Terry Pulse saying that 20 ounces of Aloe juice was administered orally to 69 AIDS patients. This juice was specially processed to contain a stabilized amount of the substance acemannan (or Polymannoactate). All patients treated were classified as hopeless cases. After treatment, Dr. Pulse reported that 81% "returned to their standard energy levels; their symptoms disappeared almost completely."

A conclusion from Dr. Pulse's data was that **the pure Aloe liquid is just as effective as the freeze dried drug made from it.** However, the proper form of Aloe Vera juice must be used for these kinds of results.

Note: Almost all of the Aloe Vera products on the market are made solely from the inner gel of the plant. *The healing ingredients listed above come from the rind and sap, and not the gel.* Therefore, it is **essential** that the juice contain this portion, and preferably, all three parts of the leaf—sap, rind, and gel. Aloe is mostly water. Therefore, beneficial preparations contain small amounts of the three important components.

ALOE-ACE™

A new standardized concentrate of Aloe Vera called Aloe-Ace contains 4 ounces of concentrate which will make 132 ounces (a gallon) of 100% pure Aloe Vera juice, when diluted with liquid.

This organically grown product contains the rind, sap and gel. The whole leaf of the plant is used, which contains all the beneficial agents listed previously, including acemannan.

Suggested Dosage: for internal use, 1/2 capful in 8 ounces of one's favorite juice or water, twice a day, either on an empty stomach or with meals. For more severe infections, 1 to 1 1/2 capfuls 3 times a day is suggested.

---

* See book *Aloe: Myth, Magic, Medicine*, pages 70 and 163, by Odus Hennessee and Bill R. Cook.

The product may also be used topically, on various lesions, including KS, Herpes, and Staphylococcus, at full strength. You may have to ask your local health food store to order Aloe-Ace for you.

(See page 85 for source.)

Omega 3 (Flaxseed Oil)

This is also known as Linseed Oil, or Linoleic Acid. It restores Immuno-Globulin. Take 1 tablespoon daily of Omega 3 (its brand name.) Buy only fresh, date-coded oil in a non-transparent container which is kept in the refrigerated section of the store. A reputable and widely-available brand is Spectrum Naturals. Store oil refrigerated at home, and use within 6 weeks after opening. Fresh oil should have a nutty, non-rancid flavor.

Raw Thymus
B-cell and T-cell Formulas

B-cell Formula: Freeze-dried extract of bone marrow and spleen with ascorbic acid. T-cell Formula: extracts of thymus and lymph and ascorbic acid. In this formula, the thymus extract contains thymosin, thymopoietin, and thymic humoral factors. This product is found to be very effective for all liver disorders.

Lentinus edodes
(Shiitake mushroom)

This mushroom is reported to stimulate interferon, macrophage, and NK cell activities. Increases antibody production and assists in the synthesizing of lymphocytes. Studies in Japan have demonstrated this product to be very effective for all liver disorders.

Kreb's Cycle Zinc

This product contains Zinc Picolinate and was formulated according to Dr. Kreb's discovery about the digestive cycle. (Enzymatic Therapy)

Thymo-Plus

Freeze-dried raw thymus plus herbal transporters. **Very powerful stimulant** which increases T-4 cells and thymus function. It has been discovered that the thymus gland secretes important hormones, one of which is thymosin. **This product gives *tremendous* energy.**

Ultraviolet Sun Bed Therapy

Ultraviolet sun bed therapy is effective for bacteria, yeast, and fungus infections. The design of the sun bed is like a sandwich: one lies between two layers of ultraviolet bulbs, so the entire body, top and bottom, are being treated simultaneously. Most health clubs and tanning salons have this equipment.

Depending on your skin type, the first visit should last only 15 minutes. Bathing suits or trunks should be worn. Of course, you wear goggles for eye protection; cover your face.

Second visit, two days later: totally disrobe, but men should cover genitalia with a towel, and women their breasts. However, for the last five or six minutes, expose all body parts.

One can vary the intensity of the exposure by opening the bed different distances, and by the time of exposure.

You can give special attention to the orifices of the body, thusly: upper lip, hold up; lower lip, pull down, with mouth wide open; the rectum and female genitalia can be spread. Ultraviolet light gets into dark places that generally get no sunshine.

The benefits of the ultraviolet sun bed are: (1) kills bacteria, fungi, and yeast on contact (athlete's foot, Candidiasis); (2) stimulates interferon production; (3) detoxifies the body; (4) pores open, causing mild sweating; (5) restores proper liver secretions; (6) stimulates adrenal glands; (7) produces male and female hormones (testosterone); (8) regulates hormonal balance.

Caution: Limit your exposure to the ultraviolet rays produced. Do not use this method to get a suntan. Research has shown that overexposure to these rays can be harmful to the body.

Also, if taking the substance St. John's Wort, also known as "Hypercium" or "Hypericin," do not follow this therapy. This compound causes photo-sensitivity while taken. Check before using this therapy when taking any substances which cause this photo-sensitive condition.

"Hydrosonic" Therapy

Bubblestar is a unique hydrosonic device that can be utilized in the bathtub. This unit is effective in reestablishing the body's balance, normalizing the bodily functions, and enhancing the natural healing and restorative powers which the body possesses.

Homeostasis is achieved through specific frequencies that resonate in the bath water and penetrate deeply into the body. The frequencies are naturally potentiated by the impact of millions of microscopic bubbles against the skin. Research on this effect, called cavitation, began 30 years ago when Japanese scientists were investigating the healing properties of Japan's natural hot springs. The presence of natural frequencies was discovered in the waters and Bubblestar was developed to duplicate this beneficial effect. These frequencies are not present in conventional whirlpools and hot tubs.

During the past six years, Japanese doctors and hospitals have accepted and utilized Bubblestar for the treatment of a wide spectrum of disorders, including arthritis, angina, whiplash, high blood pressure, insomnia, and immuno-suppression. Specifically, for the immune suppressed individual, Bubblestar can offer these benefits:

- Increasing circulation of the blood, lymphatic and bodily fluids. The metabolism is raised with improved assimilation, digestion, and elimination.
- Raising the temperature of the bone marrow from the inside out and (according to Dr. Yoshiyuki Ono, Doctor of Preventive Medicine, Nagoya University) increasing the number of leukocytes in the blood.
- Opening blocked channels in the acupuncture meridians, stimulating the body's natural healing powers.
- Massaging, rejuvenating and detoxifying tissue. (According to Japanese information, Micro-massaging takes place at a cellular level.)
- Relaxing and relieving tension, muscular stiffness, and bodily stress, symptoms which usually accompany immuno-suppression.

The Bubblestar unit can be very effective in compensating for two conditions which usually accompany and help perpetuate immuno-suppressive disorders: lack of exercise and an unconscious mind programmed to believe that the body is sick. For the immune suppressed individual with limited physical activity, Bubblestar, with little or no effort, can bring stimulation, increased circulation and all the associated benefits which are vital to the body's natural healing process.

Chronic illness tends to imprint belief in itself on the unconscious mind, which can propagate the malady. While the imprinted unconscious is directing the bodily functions to contract and close down, Bubblestar can counter the unconscious directive by influencing the bodily functions, causing expansion, openness, and ultimately, healing.

Japanese health professionals have had many years of clinical experience with the "hydrosonic" effect produced by Bubblestar. Dr. Yoshiyuki Ono has written: "It relates to the rejuvenation of cells and affects the efficient action of the hormonal and autonomic nervous systems. . . . Usage of this product can normalize and regulate basic physiological actions in the body, such as circulatory, respiratory, and digestive functions. . . . Documented individuals who were constitutionally weak and lifeless, or in poor physical condition, got well." Hideo Ninomiya, Doctor of Medicine, Kurume University Medical Department, has written, "the man-made 'hot water of bubbles' will have a great influence upon the treatment of diseases in the future . . ."

Bubblestar is now available in the United States. Contact the author for information concerning the manufacturer.

Ozone Therapies

From Europe, and in growing numbers in the U. S., immune suppressed individuals are reporting dramatic regressions of their symptoms using ozone therapies. The ozone is administered in drinking water, via insufflation (rectally) or intravenously. Special machines are available for producing medical grade ozone for the purposes mentioned above, although they can be legally sold in the U. S. only for the function of ozonating water. There is ample clinical data from Germany attesting to the efficacy of this therapy for AIDS patients.

2

HIV* "Positive" to "Negative"
Is Possible

*(Human Immuno-Suppressive Virus)

Testing "antibody positive" does not mean that one has AIDS, but only that he has been exposed to the AIDS virus.

"What about a healthy person who tests 'positive' for AIDS virus antibodies? Assuming that a 'false-positive' reaction is ruled out, this is the earliest indication that the person has been exposed to the AIDS virus. However, by definition, **this is not AIDS."***

It is true that today there are hundreds of AIDS/ARC survivors who are free from all symptoms and lead normal lives. Unknown to the public and the medical establishment, some of these people are now "antibody negative" — they no longer have the virus present. The medical establishment is in such a state of disbelief on this point, that they continue to test the blood of the patient frequently (expecting to find the AIDS virus again). Although there are no absolutes as to how these individuals become HIV negative, it is a fact.

---

*Alan Cantwell, Jr., M.D., in Foreword to *They Conquered AIDS! True Life Adventures* by Gregory and Leonardo.

The author continues to search for new ways to totally purge the HIV virus from the body, thus changing an individual's antibody status from "positive" to "negative."

It is the conviction of the author that 98% of AIDS/ARC deaths can be prevented. This startling fact is based on nine years of experience on the part of the author.

Incorrect Assumptions About HIV "Positive" Diagnosis

(1) That all who test HIV "Positive" get AIDS and die from it;

(2) That everyone who is HIV "Positive" will have this infection for the remainder of his life, which will probably be short;

(3) That medical doctors have the latest and most effective treatment for HIV infection;

(4) That the HIV virus is the sole cause of AIDS.

Answers to these Assumptions are:

(1) Long-term survivors are starting to surface. The media are beginning to recognize them.

(2) There is always the possibility that an HIV "Positive" diagnosis will convert to "Negative."

(3) Most medical doctors do not have immediate access to the latest and best information on how to treat Persons With AIDS. There is so much research accumulating in both conventional and alternative therapies that no one has a complete grasp of all the information. To date, drugs, chemotherapy, radiation and surgery (with drugs) — all immuno-suppressive and toxic — are **all they can offer**. This is conventional medicine. None of these will repair the damage to the immune system, which must be cleansed and not further drugged.

(4) In hundreds of case reports, the author and other researchers have found that to name the virus as the sole cause of AIDS is incorrect.

Other Risk Factors

Many other risk factors are involved, namely:

• Individuals are immuno-suppressed prior to manifesting AIDS.

• Many patients suffer from hepatitis prior to AIDS, thus giving them a pre-disposition to the HIV virus.

• Experimental vaccines (for the intended prevention of hepatitis) were taken from hepatitis carriers and tested on groups of gay men.

• STDs (sexually-transmitted diseases): gonorrhea, syphilis, Herpes, Epstein-Barr, chlamydia, etc.

• A habitually destructive life-style, including: alcohol, drug, and sexual abuse; nutritional ignorance and the resultant poor diet; a general body and mind pollution.

• Environmental factors, such as water, soil, and air pollution — over which one has little or no control.

• Worry, stress, late hours and insufficient sleep; financial insecurity, etc.

• Tobacco and caffeine. Although not generally recognized as such, tobacco and caffeine are drugs.

• Chemicals in food and throughout our environment.

• Plastic clothing (fabrics made from chemicals) are, the author believes, one of the causes of immuno-suppression.

Conclusion: The HIV virus is not the sole cause of AIDS.

So You're HIV Positive?

1. Don't panic. Being HIV Positive does not mean that you have AIDS or will develop it.

2. Get the best possible help available.

3. Read the books *Conquering AIDS Now! With Natural Therapies* and *They Conquered AIDS! True Life Adventures* (both by Gregory and Leonardo).

4. Have the test repeated elsewhere.

5. Get an explanation of the results.

6. Tune out all negative input concerning AIDS—from lovers, friends, family, media, etc.

7. Get counselling, and information from many sources.

8. Do not let your imagination create symptoms.

9. Change your life style from destructive to wholesome. Remove that which does not add to your well-being.

10. Do not continue to reinfect yourself with the AIDS virus (acts such as ingesting contaminated semen can infect). We know that at least two opportunistic infections are spread by oral contact.

Classified "Personal" in gay newspapers often read: "HIV Positive man seeking same." Comment: because you are infected does not mean that you cannot increase the pathogenicity (the strength of the strain). Therefore, this activity is discouraged.

Remember: being HIV "Positive" is not a curse; it is a warning.

11. Do not confide in people you cannot trust.

12. Realize that you are not alone. There are many individuals who are HIV positive.

13. There are recovery procedures that can restore your health!

14. Take control. Realize that the illness did not develop overnight, and that the healing may take time.

15. Love yourself unconditionally.

Actual Ads

*Very Dangerous—(Author)

AIDS Antibody Blood Test Facts

The Human Immuno-deficiency Virus (HIV), also called the AIDS virus, is believed to be the primary cause of AIDS or Acquired Immune Deficiency Syndrome. AIDS is a condition that is diagnosed when the immune system has become so severely damaged by this virus that the body becomes infected with other life-threatening "opportunistic" infections such as *Pneumocystis Carinii* Pneumonia (PCP) or Kaposi's sarcoma (KS).

The HIV or AIDS antibody blood test looks for antibodies in the bloodstream that have been formed by the immune system to fight the AIDS virus. The test is done by drawing a single tube of blood from a vein in the arm. A brand new sterile needle is used for each person receiving the test. The blood is then sent to a laboratory where it is tested for presence of these antibodies.

The AIDS antibody test is not a test for the AIDS virus itself, but rather for HIV antibodies. This test is similar to many other commonly performed tests such as for mononucleosis, hepatitis, and syphilis. All of these tests look for antibodies formed by the immune system to fight these particular infectious organisms. Each time you become infected with any organism, whether it's the AIDS virus, hepatitis virus, or the common cold, you develop a separate set of antibodies to fight each specific infection. The AIDS antibody test only tests for HIV antibodies.

Normally, a positive HIV antibody test result means that antibodies were detected by this test, and a negative result means that the antibodies were not detected. However, any antibody test can have false positives and false negatives.

The most common reason for false negatives is that the immune system has not had time to develop enough antibodies to be detected by this test. Most people develop a detectable level of antibodies within 2-6 weeks after having been infected with the AIDS virus, and the vast majority have an accurate test result by six months.

A small number of people may not show antibodies for over two years, and some may never show antibodies.

In advanced cases of AIDS some people no longer produce enough antibodies to be detected by this test. In a very few people, HIV antibodies cannot be detected in the bloodstream, but the HIV virus may be detected in the lymph nodes or spinal fluid through a viral culture.

Common reasons for false positives include:

- Having received an injection of gamma globulin within the last three months.
- Being infected with the HTLV-I virus. This is not the AIDS virus, but a cancer-causing virus that can cause similar antibodies to form.
- Having a severe, long term, chronic liver disease.
- Women who have had numerous pregnancies. This can result in an immune response which may cause a false positive.

Some people infected with the HIV virus who do not have AIDS do experience some symptoms of immune system suppression, including swollen lymph nodes, night sweats, high fevers, diarrhea, fatigue, dry cough, and thrush (thick white coating on the tongue and throat).

Many people who are infected with the HIV virus have no symptoms, and some may never actually develop AIDS. However, they are still able to transmit the virus to others. People can greatly reduce their risk of transmitting the HIV to others by practicing safer sex practices and not sharing needles if they are using injectable drugs.

3

Commonalities Among AIDS Survivors

At one time, AIDS was considered to be 100% fatal. It has proven to be resistant to orthodox drug treatments and therapies, perhaps because it is *caused* by drugs.

Unknown to the general public, and many doctors and other health care professionals, there are individuals who have overcome AIDS — become antigen and anti-body negative. (No signs or symptoms of the disease are present.)

The first few such cases were labeled "anecdotal" by some skeptics. The media were not interested in reporting these, because the cases were not released by the medical establishment. However, there are documented cases now, and the fact that some Persons with AIDS recover, is much more widely accepted. Of the PWA's who decided to fight the affliction in a more natural way, some have turned the disease around — and the victims became victors.

Here are the "Commonalities Among AIDS Survivors" which we have found:

1. All had high expectations of favorable results.

2. Many had dealt with life-threatening illnesses before, and so had experience.

3. All engaged in some form of physical exercise.

4. After their victory, they wanted to share it with others.

5. All turned away from traditional medicine, and refused drugs.

6. They understood that there are no absolutes in diagnosis, such as the "invariably fatal" prediction. This can be reversed, depending on the consciousness of the patient.

7. All knew that no mortal has the power to determine who lives and who dies, and when and if someone will die.

8. All took charge of their healing.

9. All protected themselves from outside influences and negative reporting by the media.

10. All were patient in their expectations.

11. All changed their attitudes and developed a strong self-image.

12. All were open to whatever worked for them.

13. All studied and educated themselves in prevention and treatment.

14. All avoided stress.

15. All embarked on new paths of natural healing.

16. All stopped destructive lifestyles.

17. Many eliminated drugs and alcohol; they also cut sugar, red meat, and dairy products from their diets.

18. Many discovered their true identities

19. All realized there was no *one* thing—drug or treatment—that could cure them, and sought a combination of life-reinforcing factors and modalities. This synergy healed them.

20. They had no fear of death—or life.

21. All had something to look forward to; many changed their vocations and life interests.

22. All realized they were not alone. They developed new relationships, which prevented loneliness.

23. They developed compassion toward others.

24. They developed a sense of humor and learned to laugh.

25. They developed an inward calm, and took control of decisions that vitally affected their lives.

26. They had supportive families and/or friends.

27. Some turned to nature and music for healing.

28. Some used food supplements and believed in them.

29. Some used Scott J. Gregory's protocol in *Conquering AIDS Now! With Natural Therapies.*

30. All explored alternative approaches, "The New Medicine."

31. All were fighters. They were "difficult" patients, asking questions, demanding answers, not passive.

32. Most tried medical treatments first, but not improving, turned to "alternatives." They recovered.

33. Many sought God and the healing power of Spirit and Love—each in his own way. There are many paths to spiritual enlightenment.

See *They Conquered AIDS! True Life Adventures,* by Gregory and Leonardo, for detailed explanations by the survivors, in their own words. (Page 85 for ordering information.)

4

Opportunistic Infections and Associated Diseases:

HIV = Human Immuno-Suppressive Virus

ARC = AIDS Related Complex

AIDS = Acquired Immune Deficiency Syndrome

The major symptoms of early HIV Infection are: swollen glands (lymph nodes) in the neck area, armpits and groin area; from general malaise to epileptic seizures.

Symptoms of ARC: night sweats, intermittent fevers, weight loss, swollen glands, vague and generalized pains in muscles, joints, and bones; diarrhea, yeast infection.

AIDS: Symptoms and Diagnosis

AIDS is a disease diagnosed by signs and symptoms. AIDS is the further development of the HIV infection, with the symptoms of ARC, but more aggravated. Dementia, which sometimes occurs, is a final stage of AIDS, before death.

It is a disease that is manifested in one or more opportunistic infections PLUS accurate, documented blood assays for HIV.

Some doctors are diagnosing a condition as AIDS based on only one of these criteria: the manifestation of symptoms OR a laboratory blood test (sometimes giving erroneous results). BOTH ARE REQUIRED FOR A CONFIRMED DIAGNOSIS OF AIDS. Only 50-60% of those persons diagnosed as HIV Positive go on to develop AIDS. They undergo immuno-suppressive treatment in hospitals or as out-patients. They are

sometimes on their own, searching out immuno-suppressive drugs, such as AZT, Ribovirin, Bactrim, etc. — to use as *preventatives!*

Two opportunistic infections that can cause fatality are a cancer called Kaposi's sarcoma* and/or a rare form of pneumonia called *Pneumocystis carinii.**

"KS" is the least threatening of all skin cancers. When "KS" tumors develop internally, they spread very quickly, causing death.

---

* For further information on Kaposi's sarcoma and *Pneumocystis carinii* pneumonia, see these two books: *AIDS: The Mystery and the Solution,* by Alan Cantwell, Jr., M. D. and *AIDS and the Medical Establishment,* by Raymond Brown, M. D.

Some Symptoms of HIV Infection:

- Red to purplish, flat or raised blotches, bumps, or spots, usually painless, occurring on or under the skin, inside the mouth, nose, eyelids, or rectum, that don't go away. Initially, they may look like bruises, but usually are harder than the skin around them (called Kaposi's sarcoma).

- Swollen glands (lymph nodes) in the neck, armpit, or groin that may or may not be painful, and have been present for several months. (These may represent other diseases or conditions.)

- White patches in mouth and persistent pain with swallowing. (Called "Thrush.")

- Persistent dry cough or shortness of breath unrelated to smoking, that has lasted too long to be from a usual respiratory infection or cold.

- Fevers (higher than 99 degrees) or drenching night sweats that may occur on and off and last for several days to weeks, unexplained by other causes.

- Severe tiredness unrelated to exercise, tension, or drug use.

- Persistent diarrhea unexplained by other causes.

- Weight loss of more than 10 lbs, within two months or less for unknown reasons.

- Personality changes, memory loss, confusion or depression unexplained by other causes; visual disturbances.

THE TEN TRUTHS ABOUT HIV

1. HIV never stands alone as the sole cause of AIDS.

2. Being HIV Positive does not necessarily mean that one *has* AIDS.

3. An HIV Positive diagnosis does not necessarily mean that one will *develop* AIDS.

4. HIV testing is not 100% accurate.

5. The virus may or may not be communicable.

6. There are steps you can take to recover.

7. It is generally believed that only those who test HIV Positive are immuno-suppressed. This is not the case. The immuno-suppression comes before the HIV. **The startling truth is that most people are immuno-suppressed to some degree,** from the heavy chemicalized environment they live in, and from the drugs that they take.

8. It takes *time* to purge HIV from one's body. (As with a hepatitis infection, it can remain in the body for the life of the individual without any signs or symptoms.)

9. The HIV virus can co-exist with you and you can still be healthy. (True also of hepatitis in some cases.)

10. Now there are a number of documented individuals (see *They Conquered AIDS!*) who have converted from HIV Positive to Negative. There are others elsewhere.

In spite of private companies and governmental agencies being unwilling to invest funds in "The New Medicine," individuals are recovering their health in new, alternative ways.

The Health of Your Immune System

The health of your immune system will, for the most part, be determined by:

- The progression of the illness;

- The strain of the HIV;

- Its pathogenicity and infectivity;

- The mutation of the virus;

- Your individual resistance (varies among individuals);

- Genetic differences (person to person and race to race);

- Your depth of desire to purge from the body the undesirable HIV.

All these factors determine whether you will progress to the next stage or not.

Most individuals are immuno-suppressed before the HIV diagnosis. Again, Candidiasis infects over 50% of all HIV persons, and is involved in close to 100% of all AIDS/ARC cases. Many doctors are unknowingly blaming the HIV virus for symptoms caused by Candida Albicans, a yeast infection. In most instances, it is the combination of BOTH the HIV and the yeast cells that contributes to the destruction of the immune system. This is why the Candidiasis must be addressed first.

Take Charge!

Being HIV Positive is the perfect time to "take charge!" It is a critical time, a warning, and a *blessing*. Your body is trying to tell you something: will you listen? What you do now will determine what will follow. If you continue to live destructively, hammering away at your immune system (see *Conquering AIDS Now!*) without changes in your life, there is no question that full-blown AIDS will result. We are now talking about *prevention*. The most destructive, immuno-suppressive elements are: *EXCESSIVE USES OF CHEMICALS, DRUGS, ALCOHOL. SEXUAL EXCESS, ESPECIALLY CONTINUAL EXPOSURE TO HIV AND STD's.* You can continually reinfect yourself.

Introduction to Protocol

This HIV protocol is for the holistic doctor. It is also for the patient who:

(1) has a strong will to live;

(2) wants to take an active part in his health and healing;

(3) wants a low-cost, affordable, non-toxic treatment for HIV;

(4) believes that there are therapies that work other than toxic drugs, and is willing to use them.

This protocol is *custom designed* for the HIV individual whose condition can range from asymptomatic (without symptoms) to full-blown AIDS. The more severe the illness, the more complex and detailed the treatment. Remember, being HIV Positive is *not* AIDS.

Treatment Principles for HIV, AIDS/ARC

First, change the body environment; this involves changing the pH (the acid balance of the body). When there is infection present, the pH of the saliva and urine become acidic. The pH values vary slightly during the course of 24 hours. One can monitor his progress by testing his saliva and urine. (pH paper can be purchased at a local pharmacy. It is on a spool and is color coded, with a chart which gives you the information you need.)

All the anti-viral agents in this section on HIV protocol destroy pathogens by altering the environment (their food). Change the pH of the body, keeping the body alkaline; this changes the environment of the pathogen. Destructive pathogens cannot live in an alkaline environment. Most disease-producing factors live in an acidic environment.

The second way to change the environment of the cells is by oxygenating them. Bio-Oxidation Therapy, such as the use of hydrogen peroxide and Dioxychlor, kills the cells of foreign organisms, thus detoxifying human cells.

The third way to change the body environment and kill foreign cells is by phagocytosis. This process digests harmful germs, fungi, viruses and waste matter of the cells and foreign cells in the bloodstream.

In this protocol, we use protein digestive enzymes, such as pancreatic enzymes, taken between meals instead of with meals. In other words, these digestive enzymes seek out and digest foreign protein and waste products in the blood. They are also excellent for inflammation, which generally accompanies infection.

The digestive enzymes for destroying foreign protein are: Pancreatin; Chymotripsin; Lysozyme; Papain; Bromelein.

The fourth way to change the body environment is via lipoid substances which destroy the protein envelope of the virus cell, thus destroying the virus.

The fifth way is to restore immunoglobulin A, G, and M. This is effectively done by the use of linoleic acids — Linseed (flaxseed) oil or Omega 3; Black Currant Seed Oil, and Pumpkin Seed Oil.

The sixth way is to rebuild the immune system by increasing T-4 helper cells and decreasing T-8 suppressor cells. To increase T-4 helper cells, we use in this protocol the following: zinc, raw thymus (B- and T-cell Formula), Germanium, Raw Adrenal, Ester-C with Minerals. To decrease the level of T-8 suppressor cells, Hydrogen Peroxide (external spray), Bio-Oxidation, and the Chinese herb Astragalus. Dosage for Astragalus is 500 mgs. 2 or 3 times a day.

The normal range for T-4/T-8 ratio is 1.0 - 2.6. With AIDS, the ratio is reversed.

"What Shall I Eat?"

There are many fad diets in our society—some of them harmful. When an individual is ill is not the time to drastically alter his diet. Changing the diet suddenly can be traumatic to a body that is healing itself.

There are certain precepts to follow in basic nutrition. Two main ones are: balance and regularity.

Oriental Medicine teaches that when one goes without eating (skipping meals), it can damage the spleen, affecting the absorption and digestion of food. Then, one day, the person has lost his appetite, and suffers from anorexia. This often happens with the sick. What needs to be addressed is meal regularity.

The largest component of foods should be taken from grains, legumes, vegetables, raw salads, and fruits—as many as possible, organically grown. Then, you may add small quantities of animal protein, if you are not a vegetarian.

One reason for eating mostly grains and vegetables is that complex carbohydrates are easily broken down, burn slowly, and so stay in the system longer.

Another reason is that these foods do not contain the rancid oils and fats that cause physical degeneration. Examples: hamburgers and other fried foods. Rancid oils and fats can cause the most damage—arteriosclerosis, heart attacks, coronary problems, clogged arteries and veins, obesity. (The number one cause of obesity is refined foods.)

The simple diet is the best. The recommended foods are easy to digest, and hence give more energy to the patient. If digestion is impaired, blended foods and soups are recommended.

Uric acid and preservatives are toxic components of meat. Vegetables and grains are far less toxic. Blended salads are an excellent food for the sick. They give energy and are easy to digest.

Recommended reading: "Cooking for the Sick," in the book *Conquering AIDS Now, With Natural Therapies,* by Scott J. Gregory and Bianca Leonardo.

Protocol for HIV, ARC/AIDS

I. **Utilization of Non-toxic Virucides to Eliminate the Pathogens.**

   A. Herbal Tonic

   B. Pfaffia paniculata

   C. PDL-500

   D. LDM-100

   E. Dioxychlor (always dilute with water.)

   F. Hydrogen Peroxide*, food grade, taken internally. Dilute with prune juice, as this masks the taste.

(These are rotated)

   1. *Bio-Oxidation Therapy*

      (External Use)

Hydrogen Peroxide (35%) may be added to bath water (2 cups per bathtubful). Soak for approximately 20-25 minutes. This process eats foreign microbes on the skin surface and also penetrates deeper into the body to eliminate more pathogens. Such a bath energizes the body and helps to detoxify the skin.

To decrease the level of T8 (Suppressor Cells) use H_2O_2.

Use the 3% hydrogen peroxide sold in stores. Pour some into a hand-held spray bottle (used for misting plants; supermarkets have them.) Before your shower, spray a thin coat over the body from the neck down, then massage it into the skin. Wait about three minutes, and then remove by showering.

   2. *For the mouth*

Use the 3% solution. To rinse mouth daily, use it straight. A small amount left in the mouth may be allowed to trickle down the throat after a few minutes.

   3. *For internal use*

The 3% solution sold in stores contains preservatives; do not drink it. Use the 35% food grade, but always dilute with water.

   F. Bacillus Laterosporus (Flora-Balance)

   E. Monolaurin

   F. Mega-Zyme*

   G. Lymphatic 25* (Herbal Extract Tincture). 1/2 dropperful twice a day.
This product reduces lymphatic swelling in the neck, groin, and armpits. It is taken by itself. If the swelling does not disappear in ten days, Aloe Vera and/or Echinacea may be used.

   H. Echinacea: 2 capsules of tea daily, or 30 drops of tincture twice a day.

   I. Cell Guard (S.O.D.) Take on an empty stomach.

II. **Detoxification to Rid the Body of Metabolic Wastes**

   A. Cell Guard — S.O.D. (Biotec.) (Take on an empty stomach.)

   B. Glutathione

   C. Silymarin

   D. DMG Plus

   E. Liva-Tox

   F. Liv.52

   G. Phytobiotic Herbal Formula ⎫
   H. Intestinalis ⎬ For Parasites

   I. Colonics

   J. Rectal Feedings and Implants

* Specific for this condition.

K. Saunas

L. Mud baths and clay baths.

III. Increasing Cellular Metabolism to Energize the Body

A. GH-3

B. Ultravital H-4

C. Natural Energy Tonic**

D. Adrenal Complex

E. Km Mineral Tonic

F. Optimum Liquid Minerals

G. Exsula

H. Vitol 27

I. Liquid Liver by Enzymatic Therapy (rebuilds liver cells). Take 6-10 capsules per day. Can be taken with food.

J. Raw Adrenal Cortex (#408-A)

K. Multi-GP

L. Amino-HE

IV. Cellular Repair to Rebuild the Immune system

A. Germanium

B. Thymo-Plus

C. Kreb's Cycle Zinc

D. T- and B-cell Formula

E. Gold Stake

F. Ester-C with Minerals

G. Astra-8

H. Pure Aloe Vera Juice (Aloe-Ace recommended)

I. Flaxseed Oil, also known as Linseed Oil or Linoleic Acid (Restores Immuno-Globulin)

J. Omega 3. Take 1 tablespoon daily. Two lipoid substances used in the protocol are: Lauricidin (Monolaurin) and AL-721.

K. Acupuncture and Chinese herbs.

L. Ultraviolet sun bed therapy

M. Water: Water is the most important place to start the healing process, since the body is over 60% water. The author recommends using distilled (if possible, distilled sterilized), water with immuno-suppressed individuals. All other kinds of water (tap, spring, well water) have elements that are harmful for an immuno-suppressed system.

N. Food: Vegetables should be slightly steamed rather than eating them raw, because protozoans that live in the soil and cause pneumocystis are destroyed by the heat.

Important Points on Supplementation

The LDM-100 in some sensitive individuals causes a slight rash which vanishes in a couple of days. No need to panic.

All liquid anti-virals are rotated four days on and four days off. They are not to be taken simultaneously.

This supplementation is done sequentially, step by step. The supplements are utilized according to the severity of the condition. The patient should seek advice from a health practitioner knowledgeable in this field. It is your constitutional right to treat yourself.

———————

** Note: The Natural Energy Tonic contains copper. At the USDA laboratory, studies have shown that excessive carbohydrates in the human diet can trigger a copper deficiency, which cripples the immune system, causes anemia, and the loss of the ability to produce antibodies. Blackstrap molasses is the highest source of copper. Fresh vegetables and beans are also rich in copper.

A New Place to Look

For several years, the author has been stating his conviction that the large bowel of the intestinal tract is involved with the HIV infection and is the primary source of the spread of this disease.

Since 1981, it has been theorized that the human-immunodeficiency virus invades the body's T-4 helper cells and uses these cells in the production of infection. This theory has been accepted for almost a decade by the medical establishment, yet clinical observation shows that approximately less than 1% of all T-helper cells are infected with the HIV. Ever since AIDS surfaced, AIDS researchers have been looking for a single, miracle drug to destroy the virus, sometimes called "a silver bullet." They have focused their attention on finding a vaccine that seeks out and destroys the infection *in the bloodstream*.

Research has demonstrated that normal bowel mucosa can be infected by the HIV. Summarizing five research reports:

The Lancet, a British medical journal (February 6, 1988, No. 8580), published an article entitled "Human Immunodeficiency Virus Detected in Bowel Epithelium from Patients with Gastrointestinal Symptoms," (Jay A. Nelson, *et al*). In the first of two tests, the rectal mucosa of four homosexual men was studied. In the second test, ten men, eight of them homosexual, were studied, and the results showed that the HIV was detected in the bowel and epithelium in five of the patients. A summary in this article states that: "Infectious Human Immunodeficiency Virus was recovered from two out of the four bowel specimens for Acquired Immuno-Deficiency Syndrome (AIDS) patients with chronic diarrhea of unknown aetiology (cause). This evidence that the HIV can *directly* affect the bowel raised the possibility that the virus can cause some gastrointestinal disorder."

The susceptible cells in the bowel are the initial site of the virus replication and could be partially responsible for the known risk of infection for receptive partners during anal-genital contact.

The article concludes that the bowel is the site and the source of the infection. "The HIV causes diarrhea, malabsorption, and other gastrointestinal disorders." The writers of the article state that more research should be done on this subject.

The second source is a book entitled *Sexually Transmitted Diseases*, authored by seven medical doctors (King K. Holmes, *et al*), published by McGraw-Hill, second edition.

The chapter entitled "Clinical Manifestations of HIV infection in Adults in Industrialized Countries," on page 335, includes a section "Gastrointestinal Tract."

"The gastrointestinal tract is a major organ in HIV infection, particularly among homosexual men. Rectal tissue may be a major portal of entry and certain colonic cells can be infected with HIV. . . ."

The writers go on to summarize some of the symptoms experienced by the majority of symptomatic HIV-infected patients, such as anorexia, nausea, vomiting, and diarrhea.

They postulate that the HIV and CMV viruses may interact in the pathogenicity of tissue damage in the bowel and also elsewhere in the body. CMV, chronic herpes simplex, anal and perianal infections are common in homosexual men with HIV infection.

The third source is from the *Annals of Internal Medicine* (October, 1984, Vol. 101, No. 4, p. 421 ff.), published monthly by the American College of Physicians. The article is "Enteropathy Associated with the Acquired Immunodeficiency Syndrome," by Donald P. Kotler, M.D., *et al*.

In summary: "Malnutrition and intestinal nutrient malabsorption are common in patients with the acquired immunodeficiency syndrome. Attention should be placed on the treatment of malnutrition in these patients . . . . Diarrhea is a common complaint in patients with the acquired immuno deficiency syndrome . . . . The diarrhea in our patients may have been related to a viral infection. . . . All patients with the syndrome were underweight. . . .

Patients were found to have nutrient malabsorption that may have contributed to the observed malnutrition . . . . The gastro-intestinal tract may be involved as part of the underlying systemic disease, or it may be especially vulnerable to damage due to the large number of opportunistic pathogens and antigens in the intestinal lumen.

"Rehabilitation of patients with severe intestinal disease may be impossible unless means are found to correct the intestinal damage."

The fourth research source is an article "Gastrointestinal Manifestations of the Acquired Immunodeficiency Syndrome: A Review of 22 Cases," page 774, Brad Dworkin, *et al*, in the *American Journal of Gastroenterology*, Vol. 80, No. 10, October, 1985.

"We prospectively examined the upper and lower gastrointestinal tracts in 22 AIDS patients. 96% (21 of 22) had lost weight, and 55% (12 of 22) had diarrhea. Gastrointestinal infections were identified in 45% of patients. Microbiological evaluation revealed evidence of infectious agents in the gastrointestinal tract in 10 of 22 patients.

"We conclude that a wide variety of gastrointestinal pathology, which includes infectious agents, neoplasms, and inflammatory changes, may occur in AIDS patients. Therefore, *AIDS patients, particularly those with diarrhea or weight loss, deserve an intensive evaluation for remediable lesions of the gastrointestinal tracts . . . .* "(my emphasis—S. Gregory).

The fifth and last source to be quoted from is *The Critically Ill Immunosuppressed Patient: Diagnosis and Management*", edited by Joseph Parrillo, M.D. and Henry Masur, M.D. (An Aspen Publication, 1987.) A section entitled "Gastrointestinal Manifestation of AIDS" is found on page 333.

"Gastrointestinal Illnesses (GI) are frequent complications of AIDS. Some GI lesions appear to be associated with increased mortality. GI complications may seriously compromise the AIDS patient by interfering with normal nutrition, fluid and electrolyte balance, and mobility or by additional pain and discomfort.

"Upper GI diseases that are common in AIDS include candidiasis and herpes stomatitis, viral (hairy) leukoplaki, esophagitis, and gastro-intestinal KS."

Also noted was disabling and chronic diarrhea, proctitis, lower GI bleeding, and perianal disease, such as herpes and Candida infections . . . .

"Gastrointestinal KS occurs in as many as three-fourths of all patients with cutaneous (skin) KS. Involvement of both the upper and lower GI tract is common. Perianal disease in AIDS is frequent and may be disabling."

Summary by Scott J. Gregory: These articles suggest that the AIDS virus does reside in the large intestine, and this is probably, "A NEW PLACE TO LOOK." He refers the reader to this book, for information on colonics/colemics, as one treatment for these conditions.

Anti-Diarrhea Diet Treatment

(1) Long-grain white rice with Granny Smith apples. (Granny Smith contains more pectin than other varieties.) The apples should be sliced and stewed in pure water. These two foods are not cooked together, but are eaten together.

(2) *Spiru-tein* by *Nature's Plus*—a vegetable protein powder. The strawberry flavor is especially good because it contains beet powder.

It can be mixed with soy milk—recommended brand: "Sun Soy," which contains no sugar, salt, or honey. This food, taken three times a day, furnishes more than 75 grams of complete vegetable protein per day.

(3) Fresh vegetable juices are recommended. Soy milk may be taken if tolerated. Dannon Yogurt is recommended; it contains non-fat milk solids.

(4) Use no nuts, seeds, or animal protein until the diarrhea stops. You may add raw salads to your diet during this anti-diarrhea diet treatment.

5

Opportunistic* Infections:

Candidiasis

Description:

This condition is an insidious yeast infection of the mucous membranes due to the toxins produced by the yeast. Candida albicans is the name of the single-celled fungus, belonging to the vegetable kingdom.

In severely immuno-compromised persons, such as those with AIDS and cancer, the condition becomes systemic (passing throughout the body via the bloodstream). Over 50% of HIV Positive persons have this condition, and possibly 100% of AIDS/ARC patients. The "yeast connection" is not yet widely understood by the medical profession, and many doctors unknowingly blame the HIV Virus for the symptoms caused by the Candida albicans fungus. In some instances, it is a combination of both the HIV virus and the yeast cells that cause the symptoms.

Persons who are not HIV Positive should also beware of this condition, and correct it. Once Candida albicans invades the bloodstream, it expels a powerful poison against the nervous system, and serious problems result, even a loss of memory and the inability to think. Also extreme fatigue and mental depression.

The "signs and symptoms" are: Food allergies, hypoglycemia (low blood sugar), constipation and digestive disturbances, bloating, flatulence, diarrhea, insomnia, night sweats, severe itching, excessive sex drive, loss of libido, persistent cough, excessive mucus, clogged sinuses, skin rash, athlete's foot**, vaginal and anal itching, jock itch, PMS (premenstrual syndrome), sore, burning tongue, white spots on tongue and in mouth, heavy white discharge, flaky or peeling skin, and a general malaise. Some Candidiasis sufferers feel "spacey."

---

* An opportunistic microbe is an infectious agent that produces disease only when the circumstances are favorable. Infections occur not because germs arbitrarily decide to attack our bodies. Illness occurs because our nutritionally-deficient, debilitated bodies permit these microbes to set up residence.

**Author Overcomes Candidiasis: The author had severe athlete's foot (a form of Candidiasis), with cracking, peeling, burning, bleeding skin between his toes. He tried everything that medical science suggested, but without a cure, until he used the principles and some of the products in this book.

He refrained from ingesting allergenic foods, and went on the Candida Control Diet. He strengthened his immune system. When the athlete's foot disappeared, so did the dandruff, itchings and rashes on various parts of the body, and his extreme fatigue, allergies, and mood swings.

Candidiasis is Widespread

Over 80,000,000 people in U. S. (one out of three) suffer from Candidiasis, states the Candida Research and Information Foundation.

This health problem is reaching epidemic proportions. It affects men, women, and children. Some symptoms in children that may stem from a yeast overgrowth are hyperactivity, behavioral and neurological problems, ear and respiratory tract infection.* Children's consumption of sugar should be severely limited or eliminated.

Most women have Candidiasis as a vaginal yeast infection. Men have it as athlete's foot and jock itch. Many lung problems are caused by fungus infections.

Some individuals are bedridden and unable to function. Others experience chronic fatigue and various physical, psychological and emotional problems, even suicidal tendencies.

One study in a mental institution showed that 163 out of 169 persons there suffered from Candidiasis.

Candidiasis, a Mysterious Health Problem

Millions of patients, especially young women, are suffering not only from the Candidiasis condition, but from the lack of knowledge on the part of the various doctors they are seeing—gynecologists, allergists, gastroenterologists, urologists, and even psychiatrists. Because the Candidiasis condition is not generally understood, these women are often called hypochondriacs, or worse. They are in a debilitated state, can find no help and often feel desperate. Here is truly "The Missing Diagnosis," so called by Dr. C. Orian Truss. (This doctor has written a book on the subject, by that title.)

---

* More antibiotics are being prescribed for children than ever before. "From 1977 to 1986, antibiotic prescriptions for children under age ten increased an alarming 51 percent, while the number of children in this age group grew by only nine percent. . . . Antibiotic prescriptions for children under three showed the most dramatic increase."

Dr. Michael Schmidt, in *Childhood Ear Infections* (North Atlantic Books, Berkeley, CA.)

Causes of Candidiasis

Drugs, legal and illegal, with their toxic side effects, and especially antibiotics, destroy the intestinal flora and weaken the immune system.

Some foods are also causes. Take a look at the typical American diet. It is low in fiber, low in high quality protein (assimilable and utilizable), extremely high in sugars, refined carbohydrates and fats. It is a deficient diet.

Due to poor food combining (mixing sugars and proteins, starches and proteins, carbohydrates and sugars, etc.) digestion is interrupted.

The best diet depends on the condition of the individual. Some persons do better on a *low carbohydrate diet* (small quantities of animal protein plus vegetables) and some on a *balanced carbohydrate diet* (grains and vegetables). Both should be tested by the individual and his holistic practitioner.

Candidiasis is an imbalance, with an overpowering growth of disease-producing yeast. The beneficial intestinal bacteria are not functioning normally, due to the antibiotics, wrong foods, etc., put into the body.

Many individuals have Candidiasis symptoms without having the yeast overgrowth. Food allergies and environmental sensitivity can initiate and imitate symptoms like those of Candidiasis.

Some individuals benefit from taking live lactobacillus acidophilus, *bulgaris bifidus* with each meal (three tablets or capsules). Trial and error may be used by the patient, to discover if this product is beneficial for the condition, or not.

A primary cause is bodily toxemia, discharging through the vagina.

Many women use douches, but the author and other holistic doctors feel that douching with strong substances can kill beneficial flora in the mucosa.

One substance that may be safely used is Taheebo tea or tree-tea oil: 4-8 drops in two pints of water.

Another natural product is Strawberry Leaf Tea, available in health food stores.

The Candidiasis Control Diet

The Candidiasis Control Diet is basically the avoidance of foods that produce allergies and Candidiasis. You may feel that the foods permitted make a very limited diet, but remember that this restricted diet is not forever, but only until you rid yourself of Candidiasis and strengthen your immune system.

Here are foods and other substances to be avoided or severely curtailed:

Avoid:

Alcohol; Food preservatives (chemicals)

Sugar in all its forms, including honey and fruit sugars. Sweet fruits such as bananas, pears, grapes and raisins are the worst. Papayas are sweet but contain digestive enzymes.

Yeast products: breads, cakes, cookies, pizza, sandwiches, etc.

Dairy products: milk, ice cream, commercial cottage cheese

Wheat, oats, barley and rye

Sodas; Nuts; Mushrooms

Fermented foods. Those with a weakened immune system should use little of these. They include yogurt, vinegar, sauerkraut, miso soup, soy sauce, mustard, brewer's yeast, packaged foods that include yeast. Cheese is a fermented food and a mold, to be avoided.

Recommended:

Steamed vegetables; vegetable soups and stews; raw seeds—pumpkin, sunflower (not roasted or salted); raw foods such as salads. However, the salad ingredients should be rinsed thoroughly, using a diluted solution of hydrochloric acid (HCl) or chlorine bleach (1 tablespoon in a gallon of water in either case), or hydrogen peroxide (H_2O_2). (See page 15 for dilution instructions.)

Distilled water should be used for drinking, rather than tap water or other bottled water; protozoans and bacteria exist in most water. It is best to add lemon juice to the distilled water.

Raw vegetables contain not only pesticide residues, but yeast from the soil, which need to be washed off or destroyed. Peeled raw carrot sticks are an excellent food. Garlic may be used for seasoning; it has natural antibiotic properties.

Raw vegetable juices (organic).

Food supplements.

Permitted:

Fish (steamed, boiled or broiled, not fried); grains—the best ones are brown rice, quinoa, amaranth and millet (the latter is 15% protein). You can purchase these grains in health food stores. Sufficient cooking is important; chew the grains well.

Fruits should be temporarily eliminated, but after the third month of treatment, you may add to the diet low-sugar fruits like cherries, strawberries, blueberries and blackberries. Notice if symptoms recur. If they do, all fruit should be eliminated; retest later on during the treatment.

Links Among Candidiasis, AIDS and Sex

Candidiasis symptoms are often misdiagnosed as AIDS symptoms, as they are similar. Most AIDS patients develop extreme fungus infections.

The Candida albicans yeast resides and thrives in moist, dark warm places—such as the mouth, the vagina, the rectum, and the male genital areas. The excessive sexual activities so rampant in our society spread Candidiasis. It is the author's conviction that it is contagious through these activities.

Some medical doctors report that they see ten women patients with this condition for every male patient. When men have Candidiasis, especially in the genital areas, their spouses usually have it. It may be a sexually transmitted disease.

General Precepts to Follow:

(1) Stop the use of antibiotics, corticosteroids and oral contraceptives, and preferably all drugs!

(2) Change the diet.

(3) Change yeast environment.

(4) Do colon cleansing.

(5) Be patient and persevere in your treatment. Only by rebuilding the immune system will one keep Candidiasis under control. Remove the causes.

20 Golden Rules for Candidiasis Control

(1) Wear cotton, white underclothes, nightgowns and pajamas.* Plastic, synthetic clothing causes perspiration which traps bacteria; also, it is chemically toxic and harmful to sensitive body parts. Change underclothing and stockings daily. White clothing should be soaked in bleach. It is better for women to wear dresses instead of slacks, to allow air circulation to the genital area. If slacks are worn, they should not be tight. Panty hose, which are made of chemicals, cause rashes.

(2) Hygiene. Be meticulous in cleanliness. After urinating or defecating, women should wipe themselves from front to back, not the reverse. Frequent bathing is vitally important. Those women who use tampons should change them very frequently—every few hours. (Tampons may cause increased fungal activity; pads are preferred.)

(3) Follow the Candida Control Diet. Eliminate from your diet the harmful substances and foods that hammer away at your immune system. Among the worst are: alcohol, vinegar, yogurt and cheese. These foods cause immediate reactions in some individuals. Add fiber to your diet. Raw vegetables, and some fruits and grains give fiber.

(4) Take appropriate supplements that increase the immune response. They should be hypoallergenic (do not produce allergenic reactions). It is necessary at this time to set an ecological balance in the digestive tract.

(5) Get the "Seven Essentials": Fresh Air; Natural Food; Exercise; Water (distilled for drinking; daily showers; if near the ocean, swim in it); sunshine (moderately used); Sleep and Rest; Prayer, Meditation, positive thinking, etc. (Courtesy Dr. Philip J. Welsh)

(6) Avoid drugs—legal and illegal. The body does not know the difference. Antibiotics destroy the natural flora in the small intestine; these are vital nutrients. Long-term chemotherapy, radiation, corticosteroids, penicillin, etc., are immuno-suppressive procedures.

(7) Build up the adrenal glands. Food allergies are predisposed to weaken adrenal function. Get plenty of rest.

(8) Sex: avoid excessive activity. "Moderation in all things." "The Pill" destroys a woman's delicate hormonal balance, upsetting the body's reproductive cycle, and probably suppressing the immune system. It is better to use non-chemical methods of birth control.

Dangers connected with intercourse: Diaphragm creams are toxic, and possibly carcinogenic. The ring of the diaphragm may disturb the delicate mucus membranes of the vagina wall below the cervix. Latex condoms may be toxic. The chemicals they are made of, the handling in the factory, the bacteria in the air, the packages the condoms are enclosed in—all these may be toxic to the sensitive orifices of the body.

(9) Do not put anything into any of your orifices (mouth, rectum, vagina) that has not been disinfected first. Concerning food: heat disinfects.

(10) Use disposable utensils, such as plastic cutlery (forks, spoons, knives), and disposable wooden chopsticks; also use drinking straws. One can carry these in his pocket or purse, for use in restaurants.

(11) Regular use of ultraviolet sun bed.

(12) Do bio-oxidation while taking your daily shower. (See Therapies.)

(13) Hair Analysis by a holistic doctor, who should look for zinc, selenium and magnesium deficiencies, common in persons with Candidiasis. **Iridology** is also useful.

(14) Use a **new toothbrush** every two weeks. Disinfect your toothbrush with diluted H_2O_2.

(15) Use B.F.I. powder daily. Rub between the toes; use on rashes.

(16) Take Bacillus Laterosporus daily, if you find it is agreeable with you. The Candida Foundation states that more benefit is found in the second month of use, and that Crohn's disease cases need to stay on this product longer than that.

(17) Exercise at least 20 minutes per day.

(18) Women may find help by using **Bee-Kind** (see page 19).

(19) Moderate sunlight is helpful in killing Candida overgrowth. Genital areas and the mouth can be opened toward the sunshine.

(20) Avoid red meat and chicken, especially during your term of treatment. You may not be taking antibiotics, but the animals are getting them. "Half of all the antibiotics used in the U.S. are fed to farm animals. Researchers say this has led to the growth of drug-resistant bacteria that are hazardous to humans." (New *England Journal of Medicine.*)

Resources

TREE OF LIFE PUBLICATIONS
P. O. BOX 126
JOSHUA TREE, CA 92252

CANDIDA RESEARCH and
INFORMATION FOUNDATION
P. O. BOX 2719
CASTRO VALLEY, CA 94546

Because of the seriousness of this widespread condition, and the desire of this publisher to help as many persons as possible, we are offering additional information on Candidiasis at a nominal cost.

It consists of a booklet entitled *Candida Albicans—How to Fight an Exploding Epidemic of Yeast-Related Diseases,* by Ray C. Wunderlich, Jr., M.D. and Dwight K. Kalita, Ph. D. Also a Candidiasis book list, correct food combining information and other materials, all for $10.00, postpaid.

This foundation is a privately funded, volunteer, non-profit agency which provides educational materials on all causes of chronic illness. They are a data-collecting center and initiate and participate in research relating to the chemically sensitive/food sensitive/Candida-like syndromes. The headquarters office in Hayward, California houses a public library where people can become knowledgeable about their health-related problems and treatments. They provide scientific literature to physicians upon request and publish a newsletter featuring allopathic and alternative research, as well as information on therapies that have been proven helpful.
Ms. Gail Nielsen is Director.

Protocol for Candidiasis

I. Utilization of Non-Toxic Fungicides

(See below for detailed description and usage. Depending on the severity of the Candidiasis, use the following as needed.)

A. Herbal Tonic

B. Pfaffia paniculata

C. LDM-100

D. Dioxychlor

E. Mycocyde I and II

F. Hydrogen Peroxide (H₂0₂); Bio-Oxidation Therapy

(B–F) Rotated anti-virals

G. Phellosatin

H. Monolaurin

I. Pau d'Arco (Taheebo Tea)

J. B.F.I. Antiseptic Powder

K. Garlic

L. Capricin

M. Echinacea/Golden Seal

N. Mega-Zyme

II. Detoxification to Rid the Body of Metabolic Wastes.

This process is intended to remove toxins and poisons from the body as rapidly as possible, particularly in the colon and liver areas. *Toxemia is the underlying condition for most diseases, including opportunistic infections.*

A. Can-Di-Gest

B. Bacillus Laterosporus (Flora-Balance)

C. Bee Kind (rectal and vaginal douche and implant)

D. Butyrate Plus

E. Wild Yam Root

F. Glutathione

G. Candidiasis Control Diet

H. Herbal colon cleaners

I. Colonics and Implants

J. Saunas (Induced fever therapy)

III. Increasing Cellular Metabolism to Energize the Body

A. Exsula

B. Vitol 27

C. Raw Adrenal Complex

D. Selenium

E. Magnesium

F. Black Currant Seed Oil

G. Km Mineral Tonic

H. Ester-C with Minerals

I. Atomidine (Iodine Compound) (If needed)

J. Multi-GP

K. Amino-HE

IV. Cellular Repair to Rebuild the Immune System

A. Organic Germanium

B. *Lentinus edodes* (Shiitake mushrooms)

C. Gold Stake

D. Target Zinc

E. Raw Thymus

F. Raw Adrenal Complex

G. Aloe-Ace

H. Thymo-Plus

I. Colonics/Colemics

J. Ultraviolet Therapy (Sun Bed)

6

Opportunistic Infections:
Epstein-Barr

(Also called the Chronic Fatigue Syndrome)

Description:

This disease is in the Herpes family. It is caused by a virus (EBV) which is also recognized as the cause of infectious mononucleosis. It is found in Chinese nasopharyngeal cancer and in Burkitt's lymphoma. The virus hides in the B cells— important cells of your immune system, responsible for the formation of anti-bodies. When it is combined with Cytomegalovirus, it is implicated in the AIDS picture.

It grows within the epithelium of the throat, and is primarily transmitted by saliva. Almost all adults are presumed to harbor the Epstein-Barr virus (probably in the inactive form). This virus can be isolated in 20% of healthy, asymptomatic adults. **It can be found in 100% of those who are immuno-suppressed.** So, this is a very important virus to get rid of.

The primary target is in the human B-lymphocytes. The Epstein-Barr virus within the body stimulates plasma (blood) cells (derived from the B-lymphocytes.) After that, a variety of anti-bodies are produced that react against tissue cells, resulting in auto-immune disease.

They can also combine with antigens. Antigens are reactive substances, often of microbial origin, which produce anti-bodies capable of creating manifold symptoms.

Any factor leading to the suppression of the immune system—emotional stress, medications, damp climate, deficient diets, or any other viral or bacterial disease, will cause the EB viruses to multiply.

Some symptoms are: swollen lymph nodes, fevers, chills, weakness, fatigue, shortness of breath, sore throat, influenza, lack of appetite, pneumonia, etc. (These are symptoms of AIDS, also.)

Protocol for Epstein-Barr

I. **Utilization of Non-Toxic Virucides**

    A. *Herbal Tonic

    B. *Pfaffia Paniculata

    C. LDM-100

    D. Hydrogen Peroxide

    E. Dioxychlor

    F. Bacillus Laterosporus (Flora-Balance)

    G. Monolaurin

II. **Detoxification and Ridding the Body of Metabolic Wastes**

    A. Can-Di-Gest

    B. Cell Guard—S.O.D. (Biotec)

    C. Glutathione

    D. Silymarin

    E. Lymphatic 25 (Enzymatic Therapy)

    F. Aloe-Ace

    G. Echinacea Tea

    H. Golden Seal

    I. Bio-Oxidation Therapy

    J. Pancreatin

    K. Mega-Zyme

    L. Lymphatic arm swings

    M. Upside down bicycle pumping

    N. Colonics/Colemics/Implants

III. **Increasing Cellular Metabolism to Energize the Body**

    A. Exsula

    B. Vitol 27

    C. Ester-C with Minerals

    D. Km Mineral Tonic

    E. Optimum Liquid Minerals

    F. Natural Energy Tonic

    G. Raw Adrenal Complex, #408-A

    H. GH-3 (Procaine) or Ultravital H-4

    I. Multiple-GP

    J. Amino-HE

IV. **Cellular Repair to Rebuild the Immune System**

    A. Gold Stake

    B. Germanium

    C. *Lentinus edodes* (Shiitake mushrooms)

    D. Kreb's Cycle Zinc

    E. Raw Thymus

    F. B- and T-cell Formulas

    G. Chinese Herbs

    H. Thymo-Plus

    I. *Ultra-Violet Sun Bed Therapy

*Very Important

7

Opportunistic Infections:

Herpes I & II and
Hepatitis B Virus (HBV)

Description: Herpes I & II

This is a violent, contagious skin eruption. In later life, it may erupt in the form of shingles.

HERPES I results in cold sores — cosmetically annoying and painful blisters. Usually occurs in facial areas, during physical or emotional stress. Sometimes recognized as the cause of viral meningitis and encephalitis.

HERPES II: Genital lesions. Regarded as the most prevalent S.T.D. (sexually-transmitted disease). It can range from a minor infection to severe infection causing liver or brain damage, and stillbirths. Babies can pick this up in the birth canal.

Fluid-filled blisters form around the mouth and/or the genitals. These are highly infectious until they heal. They are not contagious when they are healed. Herpes may lie dormant for a long period of time. Sickness and stress can cause the sores to re-open.

In a startling U. S. finding, more than 30 million Americans, or *one out of every six persons over age 15*, shows signs of infection by genital herpes, although perhaps more than half do not develop any serious symptoms of infection.

Genital herpes is a sexually transmitted disease, often associated with lifelong, recurring bouts of painful sores. These sores develop on the genitals and adjacent areas and can cause severe health damage and even death in newborns.

The Herpes lesions may be punctured and anti-viral agents may be applied topically.

Treatment suggestions:

(1) Wear cotton underwear.

(2) Practice hygiene (frequent washing, etc.)

(3) Avoid contaminated utensils. (Use plastic eating utensils, and drinking straws instead of drinking from glasses when away from home.)

(4) Avoid contaminated people (do not kiss or have sex with them at this time).

(5) Get plenty of rest; drink much high-quality water.

(6) Avoid foods high in the amino acid Arginine, such as: nuts, peanuts, seeds, cereal grains, chocolate, dairy products, chicken and other meats, alcohol, processed foods, soft drinks, white flour products, sugar, refined carbohydrates (such as boxed mashed potatoes, pizza, etc.), coffee, tea. Also, drugs and stress.

Refrain from eating citrus only during a Herpes outbreak on your body.

(7) Ultraviolet Sun Bed Therapy

A Herpes outbreak is a good time to detoxify, because the Herpes is exposing itself. The body is detoxifying.

_____

Hepatitis B and Pancreatic Cancer

Hepatitis B is an infection of, and inflammatory process of, the liver. The three major causes are the Hepatitis B Virus, alcohol, and drugs.

It is a major health consideration for those groups with a high risk of AIDS. It is spread by contaminated blood or blood products (transfusions) and bodily fluids. It complicates the AIDS picture, and usually occurs in people with HIV/AIDS/ARC, but is not confined to intravenous drug users or homosexuals. Nevertheless, it is very prevalent in these groups.

Hepatitis B can be asymptomatic (without symptoms). It is estimated that 150,000 persons annually in the U.S. acquire this condition, and 50,000 more show symptoms, including jaundice. The main danger of Hepatitis B is that is can persist as a chronic disease with disability and ultimate death from cirrhosis of the liver.

There is evidence that Hepatitis B involvement is related to pancreatitis and pancreatic cancer.

All these viruses (Herpes, Hepatitis B and CMV) blend in the liver: i.e., they join in attacking the host.

_____

Protocol for Herpes I and II; Hepatitis B

I. **Utilization of Non-Toxic Germicide**

A. Herbal Tonic
B. H-II-L (Herpezyme II)
C. LDM-100. Internal and External Use.
D. Dioxychlor
E. Hydrogen Peroxide. Internal and External Use.
(Rotate these anti-virals)
F. Garlic (Kyolic is easier to take.)
G. Laurisine
H. Viricidin

II. **Detoxification to Rid the Body of Metabolic Wastes**

A. Cell Guard — S.O.D. (Biotec)
B. Glutathione
C. *Silymarin Plus
D. Can-Di-Gest
E. Bacillus Laterosporus (Flora-Balance)
F. Ester-C
G. L-Lysine (Amino acids, effective for Herpes outbreaks) 1000 mgs.
H. Mega-Zyme (use between meals to digest foreign protein in the blood)
I. DMG Plus
J. Aloe-Ace (May be applied topically to Herpes lesions)
K. Laurisine
L. *LIV.52
M. *Liva-Tox
N. *Liquid Liver
O. *Thioctic Acid
P. Viricidin
Q. Bio-Oxygenation Therapy (H_2O_2)
R. Colonics
S. Implantation
T. Herbal Cleaners
U. Saunas

III. **Increasing Cellular Metabolism to Energize the Body**

A. Germanium
B. *Ester-C With Minerals
C. Km Mineral Tonic
D. Vitol 27
E. Natural Energy Tonic
F. Raw Adrenal Complex 403 (Enzymatic Therapy)
G. *Multi-GP
H. *Amino-HE

IV. **Cellular Repair to Rebuild the Immune System**

A. Zinc Picolinate
B. Thymo-Plus
C. Gold Stake
D. Black Currant Seed Oil
E. *Shiitake Mushroom
F. *Ultra-Violet Sunbed
G. *Colonics

*For Liver Disorders

8

Opportunistic Infections:

Cytomegalovirus (CMV)

Description

The Cytomegalovirus is a member of the Herpes family. Infections are often acquired through organ transplants and in cases of blood transfusions.

The virus usually resides in the salivary gland. It occurs in immuno-compromised patients, and is found in 50% of the general population, and 90% of active gay males. It is super-infectious and ubiquitous (omnipresent).

CMV produces fever, pneumonia, leucopenia (low white blood cell count), bacterial protozoal and fungal superinfections of the gastro-intestinal tract and the kidneys.

There is no specific therapy in Western, allopathic medicine for CMV, because it affects the DNA.

Usually the Cytomegalovirus attaches itself to other infections, making the treatment complicated. CMV might possibly be acquired from vaccinations.

Some natural germicides have the ability to pass through the blood-brain barrier, affecting the DNA of the cells. Keeping the oral cavity (mouth, pharynx, throat) fastidiously clean and steam-cleaning the lungs and throat with anti-viral herbs, often denatures the virus. CMV in the digestive tract can be obliterated with the use of certain concentrated, specific cultures, such as acidophilus.

Protocol for Cytomegalovirus

I. **Utilization of Non-Toxic Virucides**

   A. Herbal Tonic

   B. LDM-100 Internal Use.

   C. Hydrogen Peroxide

      (1) Bio-Oxygenation Therapy (external)

      (2) *Mouth rinses and gargle with H_2O_2 several times a day.

      (3) Internal: 35% food grade

II. **Detoxification to Rid the Body of Metabolic Wastes**

   A. *H_2O_2. The skin is a semi-permeable membrane. The hydrogen peroxide will penetrate the pores. This is a process of oxygenating the tissues and killing pathogens. Recommended: 1/2 cup of H_2O_2 in full bathtub of lukewarm water, once or twice a week. You are disinfecting your body with the hydrogen peroxide bath.

   B. Cell Guard — S.O.D. (Biotec)

   C. Mega-Zyme. Use between meals, to digest foreign protein.

   D. *Silymarin Plus.   (Milk Thistle, Artichoke Leaf Powder, and Cumin Root.) Detoxifies the liver.

   E. *Phytobiotic Herbal Formula (Enzymatic Therapy) for parasite infestation. (*E. Coli, Giardia lamblia, cryptosporidium*), DMG Plus.

   F. Probioplex (Ethical Nutrients)—an excellent product for alleviating gastro-intestinal infections. It is concentrated globulin protein from whey. Probioplex promotes the growth of beneficial intestinal bacteria; also excellent for diarrhea.

   G. Colonics and saunas.

III. **Increasing Cellular Metabolism to Energize the Body**

   A. Ultravital H4

   B. Ester-C with Minerals

   C. Optimum Liquid Minerals

   D. Vitol 27

   E. Km Mineral Tonic

   F. Exsula

   G. Soluble Raw Adrenal Cortex (#408-A)

   H. *Feverfew. Liquid tincture of chrysanthemum leaves; it reduces fever, headaches and inflammation.

IV. **Cellular Repair to Rebuild the Immune System.**

   A. Gold Stake

   B. Germanium

   C. Thymo-Plus

   D. B- and T-cell formulas, raw thymus

   E. Kreb's Cycle Zinc

   F. *Lentinus edodes* (Shiitake Mushrooms)

   G. Acupuncture and Chinese Herbs

   H. *Astra-8. Stimulates white blood cell count. Suppresses tumor growth. Strengthens body's major organs and the immune system.

   Astra-8 contains Astragalus, Ganoderma, Eleuthro Ginseng, Codonopsis, Schizandra, White Atractylodes, Ligustrum, Licorice. This formula has anti-viral and anti-cancer properties and stimulates white blood counts, red blood cell activity, and suppresses tumor growth. Each herb has different functions that combine to create a powerful, balanced tool in strengthening all the body's major organs and the immune system. 750 mgs., 90 tablets.

   I. Ultraviolet Sun Bed

*Specific for this condition.

9

Opportunistic Infections:

Kaposi's sarcoma (KS)

Description

In the countries of its origin — the Mediterranean, Middle Eastern and Semitic countries — this is the least threatening of all forms of skin cancer. It is usually found in elderly males of Italian or Jewish ancestry. "KS" has been generally considered as a benign tumor of the skin, and sometimes of the intestinal tract.

However, when it accompanies immuno-suppression, it is serious. Kaposi's sarcoma is reported to accompany immuno-suppression drug therapy. When the drug treatments are stopped, the lesions regress.

Kaposi's sarcoma does not generally fit the picture of a malignant sarcoma, because it is formed from the epithelial cells that line the blood vessels and lymphatics, and seldom metastasizes into the bloodstream,

which is the general characteristic of most malignancies.

The mechanism for the formation of Kaposi's sarcoma is unknown; CMV and Epstein-Barr are involved with this infection.

The purple lesions of Kaposi's sarcoma are tumors, or overgrowth of tissues.

KS, associated with AIDS, has been treated as a malignancy. Primary medical treatments are Inteferon, Interleuken 2, and chemotherapy. Although sometimes successful in shrinking the lesions, these agents usually have undesirable side effects and little effectiveness in reversing immunosuppression, the major feature of AIDS. These immunosuppresive side effects further diminish the already low defenses of the patient.

Protocol for Kaposi's sarcoma

I. Utilization of Non-Toxic Virucides

A. Herbal Tonic

B. LDM-100, orally

C. Hydrogen Peroxide. Bio-Oxidation Therapy: H_2O_2 baths.

D. Dioxychlor

E. *Exitox (Smithsonite). A cationic solution (concerns the equilibrium of the cell) formulated in the 1800's by a world-famous German scientist. Known for its healing properties and recognized for its importance involving the immune response. It contains minerals and trace minerals that interact with enzymes. It supplies oxygen to the cells, purifying the blood and helping the body to overcome disease. Dosage: 2 ounces are put into 1 gallon of drinking water.

II. Detoxification to Rid the Body of Metabolic Wastes

A. DMG Plus

B. *Vitamin A Emulsion, up to 100,000 IU per day. It repairs the lung tissue.

C. Cell Guard — S.O.D. (Biotec)

D. Glutathione

E. Extra A-Plus: 4 types of Vitamin A combined—Beta Carotene, Lemon Grass, Palmitate, and Fish Oil.

F. Aloe-Ace (May be applied topically to KS lesions.)

G. The Cancer Control Diet. (Predominantly meatless/macrobiotic/vegetarian.)

H. Hoxsey–The famous Hoxsey herbal formula for cancer. This has been used for cancer for 40 years, and is still used at the Bio-Medical Center, Tijuana, Mexico (Mildred Nelson, R.N., Director). This tincture can be applied to Kaposi's sarcoma.

I. Colonics; rectal feedings and implantations; saunas; sulphur springs* (very good for skin disorders and infections.)

III. Increasing Cellular Metabolism to Energize the Body

A. Ester-C with Minerals

B. GH-3 or Ultravital H-4

C. Exsula

D. Km Potassium Mineral Tonic

E. Vitol 27

F. Optimum Liquid Minerals

G. Raw Adrenal Complex (#403—Enzymatic Therapy)

IV. Cellular Repair to Rebuild the Immune System

A. Gold Stake Salve

B. Germanium

C. Kreb's Cycle Zinc

D. B- and T-cell Formulas

E. *GLA-125—similar to Primrose Oil. It is used as a general immune modulator and anti-inflammant. It is also successful for the treatment of skin disorders such as dermatitis by providing necessary essential fatty oils. Dosage: 1000 mgs. per day.

F. *Lentinus edodes* Shiitake Mushroom Extract.

G. *Composition A ⎤ Chinese

H. *Zedoria ⎦ herb formulas

---

* Specific for this condition.

10

Opportunistic Infections:

Pneumocystis Carinii Pneumonia

(PCP)

Description:

This is a rare form of pneumonia, and a major opportunistic infection that develops with AIDS. It is a lung infection, probably from a protozoal parasite. Patients are first immuno-suppressed.

The *Pneumocystis Carinii* pneumonia and Cytomegalovirus infection are the most frightening aspects of the AIDS epidemic. PCP is the leading cause of AIDS-related deaths.

Facts about the drug Pentamidine

(The following are extracts from a report provided by the National Institute of Allergy and Infectious Diseases.)

Caused by a one-celled organism, PCP is characterized by fever, dry cough and shortness of breath. In its most advanced form, PCP prevents the transport of oxygen from inhaled air into the blood, lowering blood oxygen to dangerous or fatal levels.

Almost 70 percent of all new AIDS cases are diagnosed with PCP.

What is PCP prophylaxis?
Several drugs or drug combinations, including aerosolized Pentamidine and trimethoprim/sulfamethoxazole are being evaluated by clinical investigators for effectiveness in PCP prophylaxis.

What is Pentamidine?
A drug approved in an injectable form for the treatment of PCP since 1984.

Does Pentamidine cure AIDS?
No, Pentamidine has no effect on HIV.

What is aerosolized Pentamidine?
It is Pentamidine diluted with sterile preservative-free water, that is inhaled by mouth using a nebulizer.

What are the most common adverse reactions to aerosolized Pentamidine?
Coughing, wheezing, burning of the throat, bitter taste and fatigue during inhalation.

What are the risks of Pentamidine?
The three main risks from the toxicity of this drug are: damage to the kidneys, pancreas or bone marrow.

The report states that the inhaled Pentamidine produces a much lower blood concentration than injected Pentamidine; thus, it is less toxic and the side effects are less.

Protocol for *Pneumocystis Carinii* Pneumonia (PCP)

I. **Utilization of Non-toxic Virucides**

A. Herbal Tonic

B. LDM-100, taken orally.

C. Hydrogen Peroxide, internally, 35% food grade.

D. Hydrogen Peroxide, externally (Bio-Oxidation Therapy.)

E. *Isatis 6

F. Hydrogen Peroxide, external use: Soak a small towel in 3% Hydrogen Peroxide and place over chest. Leave on 3-5 minutes.

G. Hydrogen Peroxide: Place 1 teaspoon H_2O_2 (3% in 1/4 cup of water) and bring to a boil, after which you inhale the steam. Discontinue inhaling H_2O_2 if you become dizzy.

II. **Detoxification to Rid the Body of Metabolic Wastes**

A. *Ephedra Tea ventilates the lungs, assists breathing, and dilates the bronchii.

B. White Oil. This is an Ayurvedic (E. Indian) medicine for reducing infection. It is a powerful herbal concentrate that can be used for lung decongestion in a vaporizer. Can also be taken orally.

C. *Hot lemonade with ginger helps to ventilate the lungs and make breathing easier.

D. Cell Guard. (S.O.D.) (Biotec.)

E. Glutathione

F. DMG Plus.

G. Pancreatic Enzymes. Take between meals. Not for digestion, but for attacking foreign protein in the blood.

H. Liva-Tox. An herbal preparation to help cleanse the liver. Dosage: 2-3 tablets per day.

I. Liquid Liver. strengthens the liver function. Dosage: 6-10 capsules per day.

J. *Vitamin A Emulsion. It repairs the lung tissue. Use up to 100,000 IU per day.

K. *Beta-Carotene. Non-toxic form of Vitamin A. Can be taken 25-50,000 IU per day.

L. Colonics and rectal feedings.

*Specific for this condition.

III. Increasing Cellular Metabolism to Energize the Body

A. Ultravital H-4

B. Km Mineral Tonic

C. Exsula

D. Vitol 27

E. Germanium

F. Optimum Liquid Minerals

G. Ester-C with Minerals
(High doses—4,000 - 5,000 mgs.)

H. *Bio-Flavinoids. These are a component of Vitamin-C complex. Very important in collagen production and healing of infected tissue.

H. Multi-GP

I. Amino-HE

IV. Cellular Repair to Rebuild the Immune System

A. Kreb's Cycle Zinc
1-2 tablets (500 to 1000 mgs per day)

B. Raw Thymus together with Raw Lung Tissue*

C. Gold Stake

D. Aloe-Ace

E. Bacillus Laterosporus
(Flora-Balance)
(should rinse mouth with this).

F. *Ultraviolet Sun Bed Therapy

*Specific for this condition.

11

Opportunistic Infections

Staphylococcus Infection

Streptococcus Infection

Description:

Staphylococcus is carried on the anterior nostrils of about 30% of all adults, and on the skin of 20% of healthy adults. It is very commonly found in hospitals. Staphylococcus is present on contaminated food, and caused by the ingestion of such food.

Another cause is immuno-suppression. Radiation, chemotherapy, and other immuno-suppressive treatments are causes.

The site or location of the Staphylococcus infection determines its clinical name. For example: abscesses (can be anywhere); carbuncles and furuncles (usually on the neck); gastroenteritis (the gut); and pneumonia (usually the lungs).

Description:

The Streptococcus is classified as microbial, according to its characteristics. The disease can be divided into three broad stages:

(1) the carrier stage, in which the patient harbors the infection without apparent illness;

(2) acute illness, caused by Streptococcal invasion of the tissue; and

(3) the last stage, which is delayed, non-suppurative, an inflammatory state.

The most common type of Streptococcus manifests in a sore throat, fever, a red pharynx, and Chore (St. Vitus' Dance).

Staphylococcus infection of the skin thrives on oil. The first step in treating this infection is to rid the skin of oil. Then use the herb called Oregon Grape Root Tincture; this is very effective against staphylococcus infection. Apply to the skin with a dropper. Another effective natural remedy is the application of diluted, raw apple cider vinegar on the areas affected. This creates an unfriendly environment for the microbes to thrive.

A correspondent had a staphylococcus infection on the face and eyelids for five years. An allopathic medical doctor prescribed cortisone, but this drug only made it worse. She discovered the herb Oregon Grape Root Tincture, applied it topically, and in a very short time, all the serious skin problems had disappeared.

Protocol for Staphylococcus Infection

I. **Utilization of Non-Toxic Virucides**

A. *Herbal Tonic

B. LDM-100. Use internally and externally.

C. Hydrogen Peroxide. Internally and externally. Bio-Oxidation Therapy.

D. Echinacea. Use internally.

E. *Intenzyme (Enzymatic Therapy). Infection fighter.

F. *Inflazyme (American Biologics). Infection fighter. Use either one.

G. *Oxyquinoline-Sulphate. Homeopathic preparation; can be applied topically and taken internally. It can cause a slight diarrhea. Must be put into capsules for internal use. Persons allergic to sulphur should not take this product.

II. **Detoxification to Rid the Body of Metabolic Wastes.**

A. Cell Guard S.O.D. (Biotec)

B. Ester-C with Minerals

C. Vitamin A and Emulsified A.

D. Vitamin E. (400 mgs.) Vitamins C and E oxygenate the cells.

E. Bacillus Laterosporus (Flora-Balance)

F. Saunas

G. Colonics

H. *Rectal feedings and implants with chlorophyll.

I. *Clay baths. Clay has been used for hundreds of years for skin diseases, because of its antiseptic properties. Clay poultices pull toxins out of the body.

J. Mud baths. Most health retreats now have mud baths.

K. *Fasting. Juice fasts help detoxify the body and break down the foreign bacteria.

L. *Chlorophyll baths. Chlorophyll is a powerful prophylactic agent. It is readily available in health food stores.

(Dairy products should be severely limited or eliminated at this time of cleansing and detoxifying.)

III. **Increasing Cellular Metabolism to Energize the Body.**

A. Detoxifying herbs: Pau d'Arco, Echinacea, Yellow Dock Root, Chaparral, Red Clover, Burdock Root, Suma, Cayenne, Golden Seal. Make a tea of these (one at a time) and drink in the evening.

B. Exsula

C. Vitol 27

IV. **Cellular Repair to Rebuild the Immune System.**

A. Kreb's Cycle Zinc

B. Shiitake Mushrooms

C. *Thymo-Plus

D. Germanium

E. Aloe-Ace (May rinse mouth with this.)

F. Use the ultraviolet sun bed.

*Specific for this condition.

Protocol for Streptococcus Infection

I. **Utilization of Non-toxic Germicides or Microbials**

   A. *Herbal Tonic

   B. LDM-100

   C. Dioxychlor

   D. Hydrogen Peroxide; take internally, and/or gargle (3% solution).

II. **Detoxification to Rid the Body of Metabolic Wastes**

   A. Cell Guard—S.O.D. (Biotec)

   B. Vitamin B-15, Vitamin D

   C. Silymarin

   D. DMG Plus

   E. Pancreatin Enzymes between meals

   F. *Bee Propolis. This substance, secreted by bees, has a natural antibiotic effect.

   G. Vitamin A/Beta Carotene (vegetable source); Vitamin Palmitate (synthetic source); Emulsified A (from fish oil); Vitamin A from Lemon Grass (herbal source).

   H. Ester-C with Minerals

   I. Aloe-Ace (May be used to rinse the mouth.)

III. **Increasing Cellular Metabolism to Energize the Body**

   A. Natural Energy Tonic

   B. Raw Adrenal Complex

   C. Exsula

   D. Km Mineral Tonic

   E. Vitol 27

   F. Optimum Liquid Minerals

IV. **Cellular Repair to Rebuild the Immune System**

   A. Germanium

   B. T- and B-cell Formulas

   C. Thymo-Plus

   D. Kreb's Cycle Zinc

   E. Acupuncture and Chinese Herbs

   F. Use the ultraviolet sun bed (open mouth for ultraviolet rays to reach the throat: 2-3 minutes).

*Specific for this condition

12

New Perspectives

Adulteration in Treatments Ill Advised

There are many doctors (medical and holistic) who have good intentions, but make the mistake of mixing dangerous drugs with natural products. This is not in accord with "The New Medicine."

Does it make sense to add more toxins (drugs) to a sick or diseased body which is not eliminating or detoxifying? Drugs are always toxic.

Our Chemical World

All persons have an accumulation of chemical toxins and metabolic wastes in their cells, because of the totally chemical environment of modern life. Everything in our environment is treated with harmful chemicals, including the paper this book is printed on. (See pages on dioxins.)

Detoxification Necessary

These are basic biological functions: ingesting food, digestion, assimilation, and elimination (expelling metabolic wastes via the breath, sweat, urine and feces). All wastes are not released through these natural processes. We recommend enemas, colonics, saunas, etc.—to assist the body in the detoxification process. Often, pains in the body are the accumulation of trapped metabolic wastes.

Three Medical Errors

The first error of some medical doctors is giving dangerous drugs to the sick.

The second error is mixing drugs and natural products.

A third error committed by doctors is shown by the following example.

A patient, HIV Positive with ARC for eight years, went to a holistic M.D. in Los Angeles with a large AIDS clientele. Upon recommendation, the patient took garlic, germanium, hydrogen peroxide, etc.—all products reported to be good for the immune system. But the patient could not tolerate any of these supplements because of malabsorption and allergies. They made her sick, and her body rejected them.

This doctor had good intentions, but did not consider the specific needs of the patient. He was not aware of individual differences or the patient's ability or inability to digest and assimilate these products, and also did not know about the sequence of treatment required, explained in this book. The doctor was treating a syndrome (HIV) randomly, not treating an individual with specific problems.

Primary symptoms are those which should be addressed first. In this case, the allergies were primary, not the HIV. The doctor *did know* that the patient had allergies and malabsorption.

Sequential Order

The sequential order of treatment is extremely important. The author/consultant would have addressed the allergies of the patient first. The common belief is that upon HIV diagnosis, there is an urgency that the HIV condition be immediately treated.

The protocol in this book is basically for persons who have general symptoms of a specific condition, or are HIV Positive *without* symptoms. The latter can treat themselves with the guidance of this manual.

However, the Protocol for Opportunistic Infections in this book is but a general guide. The health practitioner must be attuned to the specific needs of the patient.

Attunement to Patient's Needs

How does the doctor become attuned? The holistic doctor, as well as the medical doctor, uses tests. Both of them use:
A. Experience
B. Intuition
C. Perseverance
D. Sensitivity
E. Trial and Error
F. Resources
G. Research: Cause/Effects
H. Education; Specialization

One problem with orthodox medicine today is that doctors do not have the time to explore thoroughly these avenues of attunement. Some medical doctors have only a few minutes for each patient. And, of course, they are educated mostly in chemical medicine and the germ theory, which is limitation in itself.

Some persons with AIDS are committing suicide today, out of desperation. HIV individuals who do not have AIDS, but believe they are one and the same, are also tragically taking their lives.

DDI

DDI (dideoxyinosine or Videx) is a new antiviral drug federally approved for HIV, as of October 9, 1991. The manufacturer is Bristol-Meyers Squibb. DDI has many similarities to AZT. Both are *maintenance* drugs; that is, they at best slow progression of HIV infection, but do not eradicate or eliminate the infection. Neither is a cure for AIDS. DDI appears to have a different toxicity from AZT.

Unfortunately, one of its side effects can be fatal in rare circumstances, and it thus requires careful monitoring. Whether it works as well as, better than, or less well than AZT is truly not yet known. The most common side effects of DDI reported in the Phase 1 studies are increased uric acid levels, headaches and insomnia. The most serious DDI toxicities noted have occurred at the highest dose levels—painful nerve damage in the feet (peripheral neuropathy), some decrease in pancreatic functioning, diarrhea and stomach distress.

Research protocols are continuing nationwide. Physicians and patients may call 800-662-7999 between 8:30 a.m. and 5:00 p.m. EST for information and assistance.

Project Inform has literature on DDI. Address: 347 Delores, Suite 301, San Francisco, CA 94110. Telephone: 800-334-7422 (California) and 800-822-7422 (National) and also 415-558-9051.

AZT, Compound "Q", and Cocaine

Persons with AIDS are taking dangerous drugs such as AZT (legally) and a new substance called Compound "Q" (illegally). Many victims have needlessly died of Compound "Q"—while waiting for a "single cure" for AIDS from the drug companies.

They hear about Compound "Q," obtain it illegally, but it kills them. Compound "Q" possibly kills the virus (its efficacy and toxicity are still being tested, slowly)—but of what advantage is that if it also kills the patient? (One might say that AZT is "slow death," Compound "Q," "fast death.")

The seriously ill need higher aims. Should the aim of the ill be merely to kill any viruses residing in their bodies, or to educate themselves and to achieve super health? Unfortunately, many patients want only immediate relief from pain and suffering, and do not want to learn new lifestyles of prevention.

Compound "Q" is derived from the wild Chinese cucumber root, called in Latin *Trichosanthes kirilowii*, and in Chinese *Tian hua fen*. In China this powerful extract has been used for hundreds of years for abortion.

In prescribed dosages, the herb *Trichosanthes* itself is not harmful, but when the anti-viral constituent is extracted by itself, it becomes extremely toxic.

The case of cocaine is correlative. In the Andes, the coca leaf is used by the native people as a tonic and medicine. But the Western world discovered the coca leaf, and in the processing, the Westerner extracts the essential ingredient of the plant and concentrates it, to create a substance that "makes the white man crazy." (See *Conquering AIDS Now!* by Gregory and Leonardo.)

"Risk of Cancer Reported in AZT Use"

On December 6, 1989, nationwide news included a story headlined: "Risk of Cancer Reported in AZT Use."

AZT is a drug approved for widespread use against the AIDS virus. The study, called a rodent bioassay, was conducted by the drug manufacturer, Burroughs Wellcome Co. (Is not this a conflict of interest—the manufacturers doing the testing on their own drugs?)

The study found that some mice and rats given the highest doses of AZT for many months developed tumors. Yet, it was said that the findings warranted no change in medical practice.

Dr. Neil Schram, a Los Angeles internist who treats many patients infected with HIV, said: "With any medication, we're talk-ing about benefits versus potential risk. Almost any medication that causes cancer does so many years after it's been given."

A prominent cancer specialist explained that *many "anti-cancer" drugs will cause cancer*, because these drugs affect the vital mechanisms of living organisms.

Toxicology studies take three years to complete before a drug is legalized and released to the public. Many of them are not completed.

Why was AZT released to the public prematurely—that is, before the studies were completed? There was great public pressure by AIDS activist groups to find a drug for AIDS. They were literally *clamoring for a cure* immediately.

AZT was released, but there was never any claim that it cures AIDS, only that it extends the lives of Persons With AIDS (but their last days are not a time of quality living).

Medical doctors cannot opt to do nothing. That is not part of medical practice, and is not profitable.

Spokesdoctors for AZT are telling the public that the toxicology studies were done on mice, but that since mice and humans are different, the effects of AZT on mice should cause no concern. Therefore individuals on AZT should continue taking it.

Toxicology trials, using laboratory mice and rats, are traditional technique. The logical conclusion is: if the results of animal research are not transferable to human beings, then why do it at all? There are billions of dollars involved.

Mathilde Krim, a biologist and cofounder of the American Foundation for AIDS Research, said: "Considering the important role that AZT plays in controlling infection, these results should not change the medical use of AZT."

"Important role"? Has AZT ever cured any Person With AIDS? The establishment states that all persons with AIDS die, so what difference does it make? Why should they take the expensive and potentially harmful AZT?

Many doctors are using AZT as a "preventative" drug with patients who are HIV-Positive. The conditions develop into AIDS in about 50% of the cases. What about the other 50% of the cases? Also, is it possible that the AZT recipient develops AIDS *because* of the drug?

AZT may be efficacious as an antiviral drug. However, long-term usage has not been studied, because it is a *new* drug.

News Item: "A federal advisory panel has recommended expanding the approved uses of the antiviral drug AZT to include AIDS patients in the early stages of the disease as well as those who are infected with the AIDS virus but have not yet developed outward symptoms. . . ."

The use of drugs is not a science, to say the least. There is much guesswork.

"The New Medicine" should be given a trial—and the methods of natural therapy, using non-toxic products.

Acemannan Helps in AZT

A compound derived from the aloe vera plant may greatly reduce the side effects of anti-AIDS drugs by allowing doctors to reduce the dosage by 90 percent, researchers at Texas A & M University reported (July, 1991).

The compound derived from the aloe vera plant, called acemannan, might allow doctors to reduce the amount of anti-HIV drugs, including AZT.

In tests, acemannan also interfered with the ability of the human immunodeficiency virus to reproduce in infected cells. Maurice Kemp of Texas A & M is also studying how acemannan affects viruses that cause herpes simplex and several other animal and human diseases.

The journal "Molecular Biotherapy" was scheduled to publish the findings in future issues.

There is a strong protest among certain groups against the federal Food and Drug Administration. They say that: "The cure for AIDS is hung up in bureaucratic red tape; new drugs are not being tested fast enough, and/or a cure is being concealed from the public." These persons in their ignorance are desperately seeking a drug cure. This will not happen. The author has no blame for these individuals. They have no knowledge of anything else but drugs. It is all that is allowed to be projected by "the powers that be."

Cost Versus Efficacy

It is a false belief that the more something costs, the more valuable it is. For instance, AZT costs from $8,000 to $12,000 per year for treatments, but no one claims that AZT cures AIDS.

While we cannot claim that the protocol in this manual cures AIDS, it is inexpensive and effective. These natural products have no side effects.

That which costs much, is not necessarily valuable. That which costs little is not necessarily worthless. In fact, it may be the most worthwhile thing of all. The price of something does not always determine its value. This is a difficult concept for most people to accept in our society, which is so materialistic. They are accustomed to put a high value on that which has a high price tag.

A Hidden Cause of Immune Suppression

Dioxins are a family of 75 man-made chemicals. Dioxin is "the most toxic synthetic chemical known to science," states a Greenpeace document.

It is the chlorine bleaching process which produces dioxins. Wood pulp fiber is bleached with dioxin. This fiber is then made into innumerable products used daily by the public, such as: disposable diapers, toilet paper, sanitary napkins, tampons, paper towels, tissues, milk cartons, juice cartons, coffee filters, tea bags, paper plates and cups, the packaging of "TV dinners" and other foods; all white papers, such as writing paper, typing paper, copier paper, etc. Also colored papers; they are first bleached, then dyed.

Dioxin also pollutes the environment—the air and the water. Dioxin use results in cancer (suspected); birth defects (suspected); and the following (documented): *immune suppression*, impaired liver function, and severe reproductive disorders in primates and other animals.

Here is an example (one of many) showing the relationship between toxic materials and illness. For the most part, the tampons women use are treated with dioxin. This dangerous bleaching agent sensitizes the vagina, making it more vulnerable to infection. A super-sensitive state results in immune suppression, and this leads to allergies, which develop into Candidiasis. Cancer is another possible effect from inserting a product containing dioxin into the body.

Sweden's evening newspaper, *Aftonbladst*, reported in August 1988, that Head Doctor Lennart Hardell is "warning women that there are dioxins in tampons which can enter the body through mucous membranes. He advises women to use sanitary napkins until tampons are chlorine-free."

Preliminary findings by Canadian scientist John J. Ryan of the Food Research Division of Ottawa's Health Protection branch indicate that dioxins migrate from paper milk cartons into milk, and that extensive consumption of "food in carton containers could represent a significant source of some of these contaminants to the human body."

Because of dioxin's affinity towards oils and fats, many scientists and environmentalists are concerned that dioxin in such products as disposable diapers, napkins and tissues can enter the body through skin oil. The environmental group Greenpeace quotes testimony by U. S. Environmental Protection Agency's (EPA) Dr. Roy Albert that there is "no safe level" of dioxins.

Data accumulating over the past year suggest tainted papers may leach measurable levels of these toxic chemicals into foods or beverages. Says Robert J. Scheuplein, acting director of toxicological sciences at the FDA: "I think we've identified the two major sources here"—milk cartons and coffee filters. His very rough estimates suggest young children getting all their milk from contaminated cartons might double their daily dioxin intake, to a level of 2 pj/kg. Heavy coffee drinkers consuming most of their brew from pots with bleached paper filters might increase their daily dioxin intake 5 or 10 percent above the average U. S. level. (*Science News*, Feb. 18, 1989.)

Evidence is mounting that the pulp and paper industries are two of the most polluting industries. The dioxins they use to bleach are unnecessary. They can use hydrogen peroxide (again, H_2O_2 to the rescue!). Also, in many cases, the natural, beige, unbleached paper can be used. Some steps have already been taken toward a chlorine-free paper industry.

Cascades in Quebec is the first company to announce they will supply the market with chlorine-free paper products. They will produce them with pulp coming from a new mill, that bleaches the pulp with hydrogen peroxide. Cascades decided to make this move because consumers have become more aware about the protection of the environment and want ecological-friendly products on the market.

Quebec has also banned chemicals in cardboard used for milk. The Quebec government is the first in North America to prohibit dioxins in milk cartons.

On the other hand, the U.S. Department of Agriculture has denied a petition by Greenpeace to drop toxic milk cartons from school lunches. The USDA decision completely ignores the fact that, according to the U.S. paper industry's own test results, dioxin is found in U.S. cartons.

DIOXIN ⇨ MILK CARTONS ⇨ CONTAMINATED MILK ⇨ IMMUNE SUPPRESSION

One way of helping people with their immuno-suppressed systems is by removing dioxin from the environment.

Look in your supermarket for dioxin-free paper products, now available.

Something everyone can do: work through established organizations such as Greenpeace, which is uncovering facts like these, and fighting for improved laws that effect the environment and the health of mankind.

The Prevention of Opportunistic Infections

Worldwide, 600,000 unfortunate individuals have been diagnosed with AIDS since the inception of the epidemic.* (This statistic as of February, 1990.)

AIDS is no longer a disease exclusively of homosexuals. It is increasing in the heterosexual population.

Causes and Prevention of AIDS and Other Sexually Transmitted Diseases

(1) *Cause:* Lack of self-restraint in sex. Never before have so many persons, including the young, been so promiscuous.

   Preventive Measures: Self-restraint and one partner.

(2) *Cause:* Insufficient personal hygiene and cleanliness, especially before, during and after sexual intercourse.
   When people are in the heat of passion, they are not in a state of reason, unfortunately, and so not considering *prevention* of infection and disease.

   Preventive Measures: Hygiene and cleanliness. Urinating after sexual intercourse is a healthful measure; the uric acid is antiseptic and also cleanses the urethra (urinary channel) of pathogens.
   Washing the genitalia before and after sexual intercourse with soap and water and also with hydrogen peroxide (3%, available in any drug store) is an excellent practice. Also, the mouth may be rinsed with H_2O_2, which kills germs on contact. (See section on hydrogen peroxide in this book.)

   The sexual spread of AIDS would not have been so rapid and rampant if people had washed and cleansed themselves in this manner.

(3) *Cause:* Non-use of condoms, or using inadequate condoms (those that break, tear, etc.).

   Preventive Measure: The use of special condoms** that are treated with Nonoxynoline-9. They also have an applicator sheath, and an adhesive band to prevent slipping off.

   **(One brand name is Mentor Plus.)

(4) *Cause:* Depending on "safe sex." Is "safe sex" really safe and what is it? One partner may be infectious, and the other not.

   Preventive Measures: Don't have sex with strangers. Set your own standards on what is "safe." Educate yourself in these vital matters.

(5) *Cause:* The use of dangerous, immuno-suppressive drugs—legal and illegal.

   Preventive Measure: Do not consent to the use of such drugs.

Opportunistic infections such as Candidiasis, Herpes, etc. play a major role in developing more serious immuno-suppressive diseases.

This "holistic protocol for the immune system" offers suggestions in both prevention and treatment.

---

* Recommended reading: *AIDS and the Doctors of Death*, by Alan Cantwell, Jr., M. D. (Aries Rising Press.)

New Perspectives

Causes of Ill-Health

We live in a world of pathogens. Daily, our bodies are bombarded with disease-producing microbials. However, our innate immune systems keep us from most illnesses—if we follow Nature's laws.

Often, it is difficult to determine in illness what comes first. Does emotional trauma trigger chemicals which alter organs, or do organs become imbalanced and diseased and affect our emotions? Or both?

Chinese medicine states that the liver is the seat of the emotions. To restore equilibrium, Chinese medicine energetically treats the liver, and emotional problems often disappear.

Certainly, emotions, thoughts and beliefs play a role in sickness and health.

In a hypnotized state, a person can manifest a second-degree burn, by mere auto-suggestion, without any cause of fire or any chemical stimulus whatsoever. (The author was a participant in a hypnosis experiment, where he saw a burn induced hypnotically.) Many persons are aware of the power of hypnosis, and the various physical and emotional states that can appear in a willing subject. (It is said that we are hypnotized or mesmerized daily, in one way or another.)

Individuals can also create symptoms of a disease by auto-suggestion. We must watch our thinking. "Thoughts are things."

Viruses and Immune Health

Modern research has now identified over 1,000 viruses that can be present in the blood. It is imperative that one's immune system be functioning properly—seeking out foreign microbials and destroying them.

Let us not suppress our immune functions with *dangerous drugs, legal or illegal* (the body does not know the difference!), with destructive lifestyles, with chemical, environmental toxins (to whatever extent possible), with unhealthful foods, liquids, and toxic substances, and finally, with harmful thoughts and emotions—worry, fear, anger, hatred, resentment, etc.

The art of Chinese medicine, which is 5,000 years old, had no cognizance of microbials (and no microscopes to find them). Yet, the Chinese principle of treating the whole body instead of merely the symptoms is just as valid in theory as modern medicine (or more so). There are no side effects with Chinese treatment, as no harmful drugs are used; many powerful anti-viral Chinese herbs are available.

A very common expression among the people is: "I caught the flu," (or another condition, considered epidemic).

Did you really "catch" something? Some microbial flying in the air, perhaps? Germs take hold when the environment is suitable—i.e., an environment they can thrive in. Yes, if one's immune system is depressed; yes, if one has over-indulged in food, drink, etc.; yes, when the body is in a weak, debilitated state; yes, when harmful emotions are being experienced; yes, then illness comes upon us.

Too much emphasis is placed on something invisible, indistinguishable, and microscopic. Mass belief states: "Oh, the culprit is out there! I am not to blame!" Insufficient attention is given to the harm we do to our bodies, causing undesirable effects.

It is only when our immune systems become weak that our bodies become susceptible to environmental contagion. The answer is prevention. A healthy immune system manifests in a healthy body.

Who Is Responsible for Our Health?

It is clear that without consuming adequate vital elements (Vitamins A, C, and E, zinc, iron, potassium, protein, and other important nutrients), without physical activity and a positive outlook on life, immunity cannot be high.

The most harmful elements are: alcohol; drugs of all kinds; excessive dietary fats and refined sugars; contaminated food and water; excesses of all kinds (food, drugs, sex, alcohol, especially); worry, anger, fear, stress, etc.

Those with strong immune systems keep them that way with proper nutrition, regular exercise, preventive practices, and a wholesome lifestyle. These factors are all interdependent, and one influences and complements the other.

All action comes from within, not from without. One must first think: "I want to exercise. I want to select wholesome food," etc., before he can do it. Thought comes first. Much of the health literature one reads omits this vital element—the power of thought.

Exercise moderates the appetite, not the reverse, because it increases the metabolic processes of the body.

We must make our bodies a healthier place in which to live; immunity is primary. A healthy immune system seeks out and destroys viruses, bacteria, toxic chemicals, etc. The weak or unhealthy immune system cannot perform these functions, and disease takes over.

The skin, the largest organ, is the first line of defense. Our orifices (nose, mouth, eyes, ears, vagina, penis and rectum) have selective excretions which neutralize harmful pathogens and keep foreign microbes from entering the body.

Many parts of the body, including the orifices mentioned above, have specialized hair cells which prevent the entry of foreign microbes into our bodies.

Modern men and women shave much of their protective hair, use chemical deodorants, and many lubricants for various reasons. These practices and substances destroy the body's natural protection against the entry of foreign microbes.

Nature has a wisdom. Man believes he is smarter than Nature, but Nature has the last word.

The axillary hair (in the armpits) and secondary hair elsewhere function in many ways as a protection for sensitive bodily areas, and also as collection traps for bacteria. Removal of hair in these areas deprives a person of this important, natural function.

Doctors often remove the appendix, the tonsils and the adenoids. All of these have purposes in the body. If they are impaired, natural methods should be used to return them to health.

Our bodies have a tremendous capacity for self-restoration. It is the responsibility of everyone to focus his or her attention on prevention. If one doesn't focus on *prevention* then he must focus on *cure*—often painful and expensive, and sometimes not effective.

Responsibility for one's health lies first with the individual. The total responsibility should not be passed on to one's doctor. Doctors have their place in health care (especially in emergencies), but giving them the entire responsibility for one's health weakens the patient and overburdens the doctor. If some doctors have only a few minutes in which to see each patient, it is precisely for that reason.

People should keep themselves well. They need to realize their own power, and first, their power to THINK, LEARN, AND ACT. This is EMPOWERMENT and RESPONSIBILITY.

There is no contradiction here. Individuals sometimes need to see holistic doctors for learning and guidance in using natural therapies.

Enlightened holistic doctors have an understanding of what type of conditions need to be addressed. With a clear comprehension of holistic medicine, the doctor can share his health wisdom with the patient.

Our Health Credo

The new frontiers of enlightened thought are discovering that diseases are of man's own making. They are the end result of a longtime abuse in the form of poor living habits, faulty nutrition, and other health-destroying environmental factors and one's negative thinking.

Man's disregard of these laws in respect to his environment, nutrition and physical and emotional needs leads to disharmony—and disease.

Natural healing was rediscovered from antiquity in our time by a number of great thinkers and pioneers in the field of health. It is a true science based on the principle of intelligent support of the natural healing power inherent in the living organism.

Lasting results can be attained only when a wise doctor, or a patient with wisdom, assists and supports the body's own healing forces, which institute the health-restoring processes and accomplish the actual cure. Natural therapies are directed at correcting the underlying causes of the disease, strengthening the patient's resistance and creating the most favorable conditions for the body's own healing to take place.

Man's body is endowed with an enormous capability to adapt itself to abnormal, adverse conditions. But this capacity is limited. When health-destroying conditions continue unchecked for prolonged periods of time, various disturbances in the functions of the organs and glands begin to manifest themselves. These may be in the form of fever, repeated colds and infections, tonsilitis, an enlarged liver, increased blood pressure, skin eruptions, etc. In most cases, these are protective measures initiated by the organism in its effort to protect itself against the existing abnormal conditions. Ignored or suppressed by drugs, such symptoms may get progressively worse or change their nature and ultimately result in chronic pathological and degenerative changes.

It is becoming increasingly evident that the present-day medical approach, with drugs treating isolated symptoms, is unable to solve the problem of the catastrophic increase in the degenerative diseases—AIDS, cancer, cardiovascular disorders, arthritis, diabetes, etc.

The conventional approach of treating symptoms with specific drugs or other material remedies, without taking into consideration the patient's total condition of health and correcting the underlying causes of his ill health is as unscientific as it is ineffective. A more fundamental approach takes man's environmental factors, nutritional patterns, and mental and emotional attitudes into consideration.

Treatment in natural healing is directed toward the elimination of the basic cause of disease. It helps the body's own healing activity and restores the equilibrium and harmony in the function of the vital organs.

Our philosophy is based on the fundamental principle of intelligent cooperation with nature. Natural healing sees man as a part of nature, subject to its eternal laws. It is a true science which incorporates all the harmless and effective therapies that can be applied in the correction of ill health. Diseases can be cured only by the body's own inherent healing power, aided by natural products and therapies.

This book (*A Holistic Protocol for the Immune System*) is priced at $14.95. Add $2.50 for shipping and handling.

They Conquered AIDS! True Life Adventures, by Gregory and Leonardo, is a 360-page hard cover book. (Original price, $24.95, now $19.95.) Add $2.50 for shipping and handling.

Conquering AIDS Now with Natural Therapies, by Gregory and Leonardo, is a Warner Books paperback, at $12.50. ($2.00 for S & H)

How to Conquer Cancer, Naturally, by Johanna Brandt, N. D., is $9.95 + $1.50 postage.

A book catalog is available for $1.00.

Californians, please add the correct tax.

Order from:
Tree of Life Publications, P. O. Box 126, Joshua Tree, CA 92252. Phone (619) 366-3695

OR

Use our order fulfillment company —   s:
BookMasters; Call 1-800-247-6553.
You may use your credit card.
Orders can be accepted 7 days per week,
24 hours per day, personally or via machine.

Sources of several products:

Bee Kind (page 19)	(800) 223-0858
[In Missouri,	(314) 221-4747]
Intestinalis (page 24)	(800) 933-9440
Sea Klenz (pages 24, 25)	(800) 350-LIFE
Vitol 27 (page 36)	(800) 488-4865
Aloe Ace (pages 38, 39)	(800) 933-9440
Exsula (page 34)	(800) 833-8940 (Orders only)

This product is sold by referral. Please mention Dr. Gregory.

Consultation appointments with Dr. Scott Gregory may be scheduled by phoning 213-960-7999 (24 hours per day, 7 days a week). You may designate the day and time you desire for your appointment; Dr. Gregory will call you.

Index

Acemannan 38, 79
Acidophilus 56
Adrenal Cortex Complex 34
Adulteration in Treatments 76
Aerosolized Pentamidine 70
AIDS/ARC, HIV Treatment 47-54
    Antibody Blood Test Facts 44
    Definitions 47
    Prevention 45-46
    Protocol 51
    Survivors, Commonalities 45-46
    Symptoms 47-48
AIDS: The Mystery and the Solution 47
AIDS and the Doctors of Death 81
AIDS and the Medical Establishment 47
Albert, Dr. Roy 80
Aloe-Ace™ 20, 38, 39, 85
Aloe: Myth, Magic, Medicine 38
Aloe Vera 19, 38, 79
American Biologics-Mexico 14
American Foundation for AIDS Research 78
American Journal of Gastroenterology 54
Amino-HE 36
Annals of Internal Medicine 53
Antibiotics 56, 59
Anti-virals, rotated 52
ARC 47
Arginine 64
Aslan, Dr. Ana 35
"Astra-8" 67
Athlete's Foot 39, 55
Atomodine 35
Attunement to Patient's Needs 77
Ayurvedic Medicine 23
AZT 77-79
    Risk of Cancer in Use 78
Bacillus Laterosporus 17, 22, 28, 72
B-cell & T-cell Formulas 39
Bee Kind 19, 85
Bee Propolis 75
Beta-2 Microglobulin Test 16
B.F.I. Antiseptic Powder 19
Bio-Flavinoids 72
Bio-Medical Center 69
Bio-Oxidation Therapy 16
Birth Control Without Fear 25
Black Currant Seed Oil 38
Blackstrap Molasses 52
Bloodflukes 32
Book World 85
Bradford, Dr. Robert 14
Bristol-Myers Squibb 77
Brown, Raymond, M. D. 47
Burroughs Wellcome Company 78
Butyrate Plus 18, 22
Can-Di-Gest 14, 21
Cancer Control Diet 69
Cancer, risk of with AZT 78

Candida Albicans (fungus)   vii, 14, 18-19, 22
Candida Albicans: How to Fight an Epidemic of Yeast-Related Diseases 59
Candida Research and Info. Foundation 59
Candidiasis
    Athlete's Foot 55
    Causes 17, 56
    Control Diet 55, 57-58
    Description 55
    General Precepts 57
    Golden Rules For 58
    Link to AIDS 57
    Protocol 60
Cantwell, Alan Jr., M. D. 41, 47, 81
Capricin 18, 22
Categories, four, explained ix
Cell Guard 23
Centers for Disease Control 32
Chart: Germicides and Uses 20-22
Chinese Medicine 50, 82
Chlorophyll Baths 74
Chromium Complex 27
Chronic Fatigue Syndrome 61-62
Classified Ads ("Personal") 43
Clay Baths 74
CMV 66-67
Cocaine 77
Colemics/Colonics 26-28, 32
    Benefits of 27
    Instructions for 27-28
Complete Book of Exercise Walking 25
Composition A 18, 22
Compound "Q" 77
Condoms 58, 81
Conquering AIDS Now! x, 42, 50, 77-78, 85
Copper 52
Cotton Clothing 58
Cryptosporidium 24
Cytomegalovirus (CMV) 66, 67
DDI (Dideoxyinosine-Videx) 77
Detoxification 76
    Program 23
    Liver/Gall Bladder Flush 30
Diarrhea, diet for 54
Diet 50
Dioxins 79, 80
Dioxychlor 14, 21
DMG Plus (Di-Methyl Glycene) 24
Drugs, Legal and Illegal 58, 82
Echinacea 18, 22
E. Coli. 24
Entoamoeba histolica 31
Environmental Protection Agency 80
Ephedra Tea   71
Epsom Salt 30
Epstein-Barr   61, 62
Ester-C with Mineral Formula 34
Exsula 34

Exitox (Smithsonite) 69
Extra A-Plus   69
Fasting 74
Fermented foods 57
Feverfew 67
Fevers 48
Fiber in Diet 58
Fitness Fuel 23
Flaxseed Oil 39
Flora-Balance 17, 22
Food and Drug Administration (FDA)
    vii, 79-80
Gallstones 30
GarlicPlus 18, 22
Gastrointestinal KS 54
Germanium Sesquioxide "GE-132" 37
GH-3 35
Giardia lamblia 24, 31
GLA-125 69
Gluathione 23
Gold Stake 37
Golden Rules for Candidiasis 58
Golden Seal 11, 19, 22
Greenpeace 79-80
Gregory, Scott J. vii, 85
Hair Analysis 59
Health Credo 84
Hepatitis B 64
    Protocol 65
Herbal Fiber #750-751 26
Herbal Tonic 11-12
Herpes I & II 63-64
Herpezyme II (H-II-L) 14, 21
Hippocrates vi
HIV: Positive/Negative 41-43
HIV: Incorrect Assumptions 41-43
HIV Infection, symptoms 47-48
HIV Positive Patient 76-77
HIV, ARC/AIDS 47-54
    Definition, Symptoms 47-48
    Protocol 49-52
    Ten truths about 48
    Treatment principles 49-50
Holistic Medicine vi
Honey 19
How to Conquer Cancer, Naturally 85
Hoxsey Herbal Formula 69
Hydrogen Peroxide 14-16, 71
Hydrosonic Therapy 40
Hygiene 58, 81
Hypercium (Hypercin) 39
Hypoxia 37
Immune Suppression vii
    Hidden cause 79-80
Immune System, Protocol   viii, 53- 54
Immunoglobulin, A, G, M   50
Implants (rectal Feeding) 28
Inflazyme 74
Intenzyme 74
Intestinalis 24, 32, 85

Intuition, Importance of ix
Iridology 59
"Isatis 6" 18, 22
Jurak, Dr. Karl 33
Kalita, Dwight K. Ph. D. 59
Kaposi's Sarcoma (KS) 68-69
    Description 68
    Protocol 69
Kidney Stones, eliminating 30
Km 33
Kreb's Cycle Zinc 39
Krim, Mathilde 78
Kyolic garlic 65
Laci Le Beau Tea 30
Lancet, The 15, 23, 53
Lapachol 22, 25
Latero-Flora 17
Lauricidin (Monolaurin) 17
Laurisine 24
"LDM-100" 12-13, 20
Lentinus edodes (Shiitake Mushrooms) 39
Liquid Liver   35
Liva-Tox 23
"LIV.52" Herbal Formula 23
Liver 23, 30
Liver/Gall Bladder Flush 30
Living Earth 25
Lomatia Dissectum (LDM-100) 12
Lourdes, France 15
"Lymphatic 25" 24
Lymphatic Arm Swings 25
Magnesium 35
Magnesium sulphate (Epsom Salt) 30
Mayo Clinic 14-15
McDaniel, H. Reg, Dr. 38
Meat, avoid 59
Medical World News 38
Mega-Zyme 24. 67
Metabolism, increasing cellular 33-36
Meyer, Dr. Theodore 25
Milk, contaminated 80
Missing Diagnosis, The 56
Monolaurin 17, 22
Mother's milk 15
Mud baths 74
Multi-GP 36
Mycocyde I and II 13, 21
Myrrh 19
National Institute of Allergy and
    Infectious Diseases 70
Natural Energy Tonic 36
Nelson, Mildred, R. N. 69
New England Journal of Medicine 59
New Medicine, The vi, vii, 78
New Perspectives 76-84
Nystatin 14, 25
Occult Stool Specimens for Ova 31
Olive Oil 30
Omega 3 (Flaxseed Oil) 39

Opportunistic Infections 55
    Causes & Prevention 81
Opportunistic microbes 55
Optimum Liquid Minerals 34
Oregon Grape Root Tincture 73
Organic Germanium 36
Oxyquinoline-Sulphate 74
Ozone Therapies 40
Pancreatin (Mega-Zyme) 24
Pancreatic Cancer 64
Parasites 31-32
Parrillo and Mazur, M. D's 54
Parrish, Louise, M. D. 24
Pau d'Arco 25
PCP 69-71
PDL-500 13, 21
Pentamidine   70
Pfaffia Paniculata 12, 20
Phagocytes 35
Phellostatin 13, 21
Phytobiotic Herbal Formula   24
"The Pill" 58
Pneumocystis Carinii Pneumonia
    Description 70
    Protocol 71
Polymannoactate 38
Premenstrual Syndrome (PMS) 33
Prevention of Opportunistic Infections 81
Probioplex 67
Procaine (GH-3) 35
Project Inform 77
Protocols
    Candidiasis 60
    Cytomegalovirus 67
    Detailed descriptions 11
    Epstein-Barr 62
    General Treatment Principles viii
    Hepatitis B 65
    Herpes I and II 65
    HIV, ARC, AIDS   51
    Kaposi's sarcoma 69
    Pneumocystis carinii Pneumonia 71
    Staphylococcus Infection 73
    Streptococcus Infection 75
Pulse, Dr. Terry 38
Raw Adrenal Complex 34
Raw Lung Tissue 72
Raw Thymus 39
Rectal feeding 28, 69
Rectal Swab Technique 24
Rejuvenation (liver/gall bladder flush) 30
Responsibility for Health 83
Risk factors 42
Rodriguez, Dr. Rodrigo 14
Rosenow, Dr. Edward Carl 15
Rotation of anti-virals 52
Rothschild, Peter, M.D. 23
"Safe Sex" 81
St. John's Wort 39, 45
Scheuplein, Robert J. 80

Sauna, Process, cautions 28-29
Schram, Dr. Neil 78
Science News 80
Sea-Klenz 24-25, 85
Selenium 35
Sequential order 77
Sex, moderation in 58
Sexually Transmitted Diseases (STD's) 81
Sexually Transmitted Diseases 58
Seven Essentials of Health vi, 58
Shiitake Mushrooms 39
Silymarin Plus 24
Sperti, Dr. George 15
Spiru-tein 54
Stanford University 14
Staphylococcus Infection
    Description 73
    Protocol 74
Streptococcus Infection
    Description 73
    Protocol   75
Suicide (Persons with AIDS) 77
Sunlight 59
Swimming and parasites 32
Taheebo Tea 25
Tapeworms 32
They Conquered AIDS vi, 41, 42, 85
Thioctic Acid   (Lipoic Acid) 24
Thrush 16, 44, 48
Thyme 19
Thymo-Plus 39
Time Frame of Teatments ix
Toxemia (self poisoning) 60
Treatment Principles viii
Tree of Life Publications iv, 33, 59, 85
Tree-Tea Oil 25
Tri-Methylglycine (TMG) 24
Truss, Dr. Orion T. 56
Twenty Golden Rules
    for Candidiasis Control 58
Ultraviolet Sun Bed Therapy 39
Ultravital H-4 35
Upside Down Bicycle Pumping 25
U. S. Dept. of Agriculture (USDA) 80
Uric Acid 50
Vaginitis 19
Vinegar, apple cider 73
Viricidin 24
Virucides, Non-Toxic 11
Viruses and Immune Health 82
Vitamin C and E 74
Vitol 27 36, 85
Walking as Exercise 25-26
Warburg, Dr. Otto 15
Water 52
Wild Yam Root 25
Wunderlich, Ray C. Jr., M. D. 59
Yarrow 19
Zinc 39